the individuated hobbit

Timothy R. O'Neill

the individuated hobbit

Jung, Tolkien
and the Archetypes
of Middle-earth

with 13 illustrations

THAMES AND HUDSON

92-948

First published in Great Britain in 1980
by Thames and Hudson Ltd, London
© 1979 Timothy R. O'Neill

Printed and bound in Great Britain by Richard Clay (The Chaucer Press) Ltd, Bungay, Suffolk.

Chorus Mysticus:

> Alles Vergängliche
> Ist nur ein Gleichnis;
> Das Unzulängliche,
> Hier wird's Ereignis;
> Das Unbeschreibliche,
> Hier ist's getan;
> Das Ewig-Weibliche
> Zieht uns hinan.

Goethe, *Faust*

pReface

I FIRST READ *The Lord of the Rings* in 1968 at the insistence of Bob Killebrew, an old friend and dedicated paratrooper who is at this writing assigned to the US Army's 82nd Airborne Division. He had been introduced to the enchantment of Middle-earth as a new lieutenant, shortly before his marriage, completing *The Lord of the Rings* on his honeymoon — for which reason I feel safe in counting him a true fan. His bride, a lady of keen wit and elfin feature, was far more understanding than old Bob had a right to expect. At the time of his early enthusiasm he visited me at Fort Meade, Maryland. I was busy at the time with the joys of command, and hardly in a position to embark on any extensive reading; when we visited a drug store in search of something or other, and he asked whether I had read any Tolkien I think I replied that I hadn't the remotest notion what a Tolkien was. He assured me that I had not lived.

Unfortunately, only Volume Two was available on the paperback shelf, but Bob convinced me that I could catch up later. He was only half right. I joined the story as Aragorn was racing up the slopes of Amon Hen in search of Frodo. I was a little puzzled at the time about the presence of a range in so unlikely a setting, since a Ranger in the American Army is a soldier with a special small-unit skill qualification who, among other attributes, sees in the dark, never sleeps, and dispatches snakes by decapitating them with his teeth. My friend was only limited help. There were too many things that had gone before, complex antecedents that made for utter confusion. But the pace and rhythm of the story, and the oddly fascinating antiquarian sound of place names, kept me going. I snapped up *The Return of the King* a week later, then devoured in quick succession the first volume, *The Fellowship of the Ring*, *The Hobbit*, and the slim selection of associated gleanings. I even read the appendices.

The three volumes, battered and torn, lived through my second tour in Vietnam. The second reading proceeded under a poncho liner and mosquito net in a bunker at Nui Con Thien. *The Two Towers* was blown clear of my tank when the noble steed contrived to discover a land mine near the Demilitarized Zone. I have often wondered if it fell into enemy hands (an enemy with a small "e") and if so how their intelligence officers interpreted it.

My older daughter learned early of the landscape of Middle-earth. We followed a ritual, in the middle of her fifth year, of nightly reading aloud. It was then that I discovered the key to the odd narrative quality of Tolkien's diction, for it was clear that much of the prose was written to be recited, not silently skimmed over. There was a meter in the best passages, and my daughter was properly enthralled, absorbed in the peculiar mythology from Bilbo's first smoke ring to Frodo's departure for the Uttermost West. She cut her teeth on a strange language; saw an abyss where others observed only a hole in the ground, found skunks noisome rather than smelly, splashed through stagnant fens instead of puddles. Whether this journey will prove to have enriched her remains to be seen.

After my return from the war the Tolkien books became a permanent fixture. My long-suffering wife was indulgent enough to saw gamely away at Donald Swann's rendering of hobbit songs on the violin, and I tried during idle hours to discover the key to the Fëanorean script from fragments here and there. My interests were not really academic, but rather the simple pleasures of escape and the bewitching attraction I sensed in the imagery of Middle-earth. In a peculiar fashion some part of me — doubtless the Celtic — was haunted by those images.

I read a number of published critical perspectives of Tolkien's work in the years that followed, and felt uniformly unsatisfied with their conclusions. To point out that the language of Middle-earth was derived from existing obsolete sources was interesting from the scholarly point of view, but certainly very much beside the real point — whatever *that* might have been. The search for comparisons between Tolkien's characters and those of Celtic or Norse mythology is a compelling excursion, and one which leaves us in awe of the author's erudition; but the conclusions should not be too surprising, since that was Tolkien's chosen field of study. Cross-cultural mythical themes and their earnest investigation do not of themselves solve many mysteries. To define God as "something like *Gott* or *Adonai* or *Allah*" may display a fund of superficial information, but yield not the slightest hint of the nature or substance of divinity.

Some years later the Army decided in its wisdom that I was to become a psychologist, and I spent two happy years of paid sabbatical at the University of North Carolina at Chapel Hill, absorbing the lore of art and science in human behavior. In the process I was exposed to the analytical psychology of Carl G. Jung. An aunt had seen fit to send me a copy of *Man and His Symbols*, a feast of mandalas and hallucinogens; but my first really rigorous contact with this school of personality theory was in a graduate survey course. This time I was struggling with Jung for a grade, and probably missed in my anxious memorization of detail the heart of analytical psychology. In any case I swallowed the complexities whole, almost undigested. They percolated in some unseen place for some time.

Following the award of the Master's Degree I was transferred to West Point as an instructor in the Department of Behavioral Sciences and Leadership. It amused me to insert an hour (an hour!) on Jung into the presentation of the introductory psychology course. This was a bolder undertaking than the untutored would appreciate. The psychology committee at the United States Military Academy is pretty uniformly Behaviorist in philosophy, and anything that does not involve albino rats and a buzzer is usually dismissed as Velikovskyan. The cadets, on the other hand, welcomed the break from two hours of Freud. They chuckled at the depiction of the Army's system of commissioned rank symbols as transcendental in theme, and rolled their eyes upward at my multicolor chalk rendering of the quaternal Norse universe peopled with symbols: domes of glittering stars, abysses of fire and ice, cranky dwarfs, capricious gods, bound together by the life tree.

But it was a conversation with an instructor in the English Department that finally brought the two passions together. He made the suggestion, during a break between events in the physical training test, that the whole Ring Adventure was, there and back again, an explicit Freudian statement. I was (and am) suspicious of any Freudian claims about literary themes, rejecting such facile pop analyses as politely as Professor Tolkien eschewed allegory. My friend was not to be denied. The residence at Bag End has, to be sure, a certain womblike flavor, but to impugn the honorable name of Baggins with suggestions of anal syndrome stretches license to the limit. Besides, literary critics, especially amateur ones, see Freudian themes in every independent clause, totem in every strong figure, and the Rat Man in every ambivalent one.

I set out that night to write a rebuttal, intending to take an adversary approach. But I soon abandoned as unworthy of effort a mere repudiation of underlying psychosexual themes. In a sudden moment of enlightenment, the tale rearranged itself and the obvious relevance of Jung's psychology of Self-realization emerged as a clear figure against an enchanting ground. I had never thought of the work in this context, being content to enjoy it without theoretical conceit for its own sake — like most of us, relishing the trip without knowing where it led or why.

The theme and obsession of the present work formed itself that very night, which was nearly two years ago. Unlike Tolkien's deity, I had no demiurgic offspring to whom I could delegate the project. Like Tolkien, I cannot afford typing assistance; I also teach a full academic schedule, administer a pool of instructors and a variety of courses, pursue research in quite another area of psychology, assume coaching duties in their proper season, and try to keep a family amused. This work did not, moreover, "grow in the telling." Rather it shrank as I realistically assessed my own shortcomings and the magnitude of the task at hand. Attempting to reconcile Jung and Tolkien is much like fondling the tail of a tiger in each hand. Sources have footnotes, and the footnoted sources have other references. Since infinite regress threatened, I finally had to redefine the boundaries of the book and sorrowfully abandon such promising excursions as a romp through the Finnish *Kalevala* and a separate chapter on *The Silmarillion*. I can only hope that the arguments I offer satisfy the discerning reader.

The most serious problem was not, however, the technical issue of source, support, and structure, but the selection of an audience for the book. The reader must clearly have some familiarity with two areas: the personality theories of Jung and the plot and device of Tolkien's works. A discussion which presupposes a knowledge of *both* these at the outset is suitable for a very small readership indeed. One familiar with neither man's ideas would, on the other hand, scarcely be tempted to pick this slender volume from the shelf. This leaves a challenge: one man's work or the other must be described in detail before comparisons are made.

The choice is inescapable. Far more Americans are familiar with Tolkien than with Jung. The latter's theories, though based largely upon religious history, mythology, and interpretation of clinical experience, are really no less full of magic than the Ring Cycle, as a growing readership in this country is coming to learn. But Jung never enjoyed the popularity of his elder-ego from Vienna. This probably spared Jung (to grope for a silver lining) the vast mythology of half-understanding, misconception, and conventional wisdom that still plagues Freud's reputation. Because of this widespread ignorance some background in Jungian theory must clearly be provided.

Unfortunately, providing "some background" tends to get out of hand. To understand Jung's theory, we must understand the nature and boundaries of personality theories in general; to grasp *these*, we must review the three historical approaches to the problem (at least superficially), particularly the peculiarities and contrasts of the two theoretical perspectives — psychoanalysis and Humanism — which analytical psychology bridges. This understanding must in turn be founded on a knowledge of theory and what we shall call *construct*.

The result is that the first two chapters of this book deal with the nature of theories and their application to personality. A great deal of philosophy creeps into this discussion, along with a few of those key terms my cadets call (with little affection) "buzz-words." While I do not intend to write a book on vocabulary, I would be uncomfortable if I neglected to provide the reader with some structure with which to make sense out of the dizzying array of constructs and dynamics that populate the wide space between science and art, concrete and mystical.

The discussion of the books themselves will center on a relatively few repetitive themes: the transforming archetypes of Self-realization and the personifying archetypes of the various characters in the psyche. The symbols of the Self — crystal, mandala, quaternion — and the map of the human psyche provided by a complex series of star-sun-moon metaphors, the recurrent union of opposites, and a variety of battling creatures of the unconscious provide one of the most fertile sources of archetype in human expression to be found in modern literature.

I am reassured, despite the very academic introductory pages, that the reader who relished Tolkien's world will find further joy (and a touch of scientific rigor) in Jung's theoretical framework; they are waters drawn, so to speak, from the same enchanted well. A few of those who have indulged in the peculiar charms of Middle-earth will ask, fairly enough: Why dissect the thing at all? Will the story, disassembled and picked over and tinkered with like literary clockwork, have any more life or nourishment than the story itself? Surely the whole of Tolkien's world is subtly greater than the sum of its parts and one who would, like Saruman, break the thing down to see what it is made of has "left the path of wisdom!"

I am not in the least guilty about this. There is, I allow myself to hope, an end result in the path of this examination that will deepen the effect of the story, make its message more lucid and personal. If I am wrong, I have at least been wrong for the best of reasons.

For those who will begin this reading with a substantial grounding in Jungian theory, I have a special caution. I am not Jung, but merely Timothy O'Neill with his own weaknesses and biases. If I have at one point or another done violence to accepted theory, it is not through malice but ignorance — my real field is the psychophysics of camouflage. In some cases I have bent the limits of Jung's specific intent (or at least as I interpret his intent) to fit the story, but I have had the courtesy at least in each case to warn the reader, and absolve Jung of any responsibility for overambitious or downright bogus interpretations. More than this I cannot say without sounding like Uriah Heep. These are my own limitations: draw your conclusions after you have weighed the arguments.

And I give special thanks to those few who *will*, I trust, read the first chapters: especially Mrs. John Trezevant O'Neill, one of the rare fans of both Jung *and* Tolkien and my wife, who put up with my reclusive writing habits and fell asleep more than once proofreading the results.

> *Then, without further circumvention,*
> *Give metaphysics your attention.*
> *There seek profoundly to attain*

What does not fit the human brain;
Whether you do or do not understand,
An impressive word is always at hand.

— Goethe [1]

[1] Goethe, *Faust*, Pt I, ll. 1948–53; trans. Walter Kaufmann, Garden City, New York: Doubleday, 1961. All translated quotations from *Faust* in this book are cited from this work.

contents

list of illustrations

the individuated hobbit

I

introduction: theory

THE WIDESPREAD POPULARITY of J. R. R. Tolkien's fantasy fiction is one of the most unexpected literary phenomena of our time. Once rejected by its publisher, and regarded even at its acceptance as a probable literary loss[1], *The Lord of the Rings* has become staple fare for high school and college students, their professors, and an incredible variety of other readers; spawned a flourishing industry engaged in manufacturing and promoting paraphernalia; and withstood the determined assault of a great body of cult and criticism. In an age of skepticism, the frenzied acceptance of a three-volume fairy tale and its assorted sequels and appendices is scarcely to be believed. Explanations for its success are as varied as the assessments of critics. The gist of the collective conventional wisdom is that the fantasy world of Middle-earth provides escape from an increasingly unpleasant reality, with all the advantages and dangers that sort of unreality carries with it.

The thesis of this book is that "escape" is too facile an ex-

[1] Carpenter, *J. R. R. Tolkien*, pp. 211–21, passim. Facts of publication, where not cited on the page, are given in the Bibliography.

planation to be anything but misleading. The idea of escape literature carries with it the implication of unhealthiness, of trivial, unwholesome fantasy, and denial of that which is "real" and hence worthy of our interest. My proposition is just the opposite: that it is the relative ill-health of our age which creates the need for the special kind of fantasy that Middle-earth provides, and that the narrow view of "reality" that the critics champion may be the beginning of what is really unhealthy.

The real power of Tolkien's world is as much in form as in content. The difference between myth and a story is just that: a story becomes myth (or, in diminutive form, "fairy tale") when a certain form is imposed on it. What that form should be is the subject of this book. The most immediate hallmark of that form is the degree to which it evokes images in the reader — images that are in harmony with the common psychological heritage of all Man.

What I am really suggesting in these pages is that there are two kinds of reality: the objective reality of personal experience and perception, which we call consciousness, and the subjective reality which is outwardly directed. The first is practical, demonstrative, and concerned with outward-looking energy and social reality. The second is inward-looking, symbolic, and profoundly affected not only by Man's day-to-day encounters with the world, but also by the collective experience of Man through the ages. The power of enchantment in Middle-earth is not to be found in this outward-looking consciousness, but is rooted in a deeper, far more ancient part of Man: a seldom-glimpsed realm "where the shadows lie."

Just how this happens has, I think, escaped the critics and cultists. There have been detailed explorations of odd place names, exhaustive searches for obscure source and mythological parallel — for the "meaning" that Professor Tolkien assured us repeatedly was not there. To the extent that there is no allegorical meaning or hidden satire, I am in agreement with the author. But meaning comes in various disguises, and if plot and content are to be taken at face value and simply enjoyed, then the reasons for the attractions must be found in form. The meaning, if meaning is the correct word, of this source of attraction is unique for each reader; each man's psyche is his own, despite strains of commonality, and will make of the charms and joys of Middle-earth what it will without the slyness of satire or the blunt instrument of allegory.

My purpose is to demonstrate that the framework of Tolkien's world is truly in harmony with "real" myth and fairy tale, that they are woven of the same strand of human psychology. The common denominator of all such expression is to be found in the theoretical framework of analytical psychology — in the concepts of the collective unconscious and in the search for Self-realization. This is the vast complex perspective of Carl G. Jung and his inheritors, a set of theories only dimly grasped by most psychologists and frequently (if unfairly) dismissed as nonempirical, mystical, and nearly incomprehensible. Although the impact of Jungian theory is considerable — more in art and literature than in psychology — its delicate mechanics (what we will call its "constructs") are hardly even addressed in introductory psychology texts. It is this obscurity which has, I think, caused its applicability to Tolkien's work to elude readers. I hope to correct this oversight.

But this requires the reader to understand the basics of analytical psychology, which is no mean task. I will freely confess that most of my present knowledge of Jung's theory evolved during the preparation of this book. What I have provided is a very rapid survey of Jung's major ideas, which I hope will be made comprehensible even after my condensation and interpretation.

The necessary explanation of my perspective requires

many pages even after (as I hope) separating wheat from chaff — "chaff" being in this case the subjects which do not apply directly to the matter at hand — and I can only hope that readers will not injure themselves yawning and nodding. I teach general psychology to West Point cadets during the first hour after lunch, and keeping their attention often requires overcoming the effects of pot roast or shepherd's pie in deadly combat with late hours finishing a history paper or girding for a physics examination. My readers are not a captive audience, however, and there is no penalty (save possibly a bruised toe) if the book should slip finally from a sleeping hand. I can only promise that the introduction to personality theory is necessary, and that its application to the world of Elf and hobbit is real and significant — and, I hope, worth wading through theory and construct.

But to understand Jung and his theories in proper perspective, we should look briefly at what a theory is and how his own fits into the broader study of personality.

The *American College Dictionary* defines a theory as "a coherent group of general propositions used as principles of explanation for a class of phenomena: Newton's theory of gravitation."

Hold a mass (other than the family hamster, a raw egg, or a cherished heirloom) in your preferred hand; release it and critically observe its behavior. Unless I miss my guess, it will fall toward the center of the earth.

Observation: A mass, when released, will tend to fall toward the center of the earth.

Theory: There is a force, which we will for convenience call *gravity*, that acts consistently to attract masses to each other.

This theory satisfactorily explains the repeated observation that things tend to fall downward when released, a phenomenon I occasionally rediscover at the kitchen sink. I feel comfortable accepting it because I have never seen a contrary occurrence. But this wonderful thing, this theory of gravity, which comforts us with the assurance that things will not embarrass us by falling *up*, becomes even more wondrous when we note that no one has ever seen or described the essence of gravity. We observe its effects everywhere, yet we may only *infer* that it exists. This does not bother us only because the effects of gravity are so comfortingly consistent, measurable, and empirical that we hardly dare challenge its existence. Yet it still eludes our wisdom to place *a gravity* under a scanning electron microscope and take its full measure. It is still only a word, a convenient label for a thing whose existence must for the present remain inferential. Such a label for the component of a theory is called a *construct*.

Constructs come in all shapes and sizes, conservative and liberal, simple and complex, concrete and abstract. Some are dry and creatively jejune (e.g., gravity); some have exquisite visual imagery in the mind's eye. Among the latter are the wave and particle models of light: visual, quasi-mechanical models, which explain and predict the "behavior" of light by approximating it in observable analogy. Light cares nothing for these models and behaves as it damned well pleases, but mortals are amused to picture light as ball bearings rolling down ramps or waves in a ripple tank. Light is neither, but its true essence is not yet to be visualized by the mind's eye.

These construct systems may be more or less elaborate in standing in for the structure and dynamics of reality. The planetary atom, with its nuclear center packed like a raspberry with protons and neutrons, circled in endless ballet by electron-satellites, is no longer recognized as representing an accurate picture of the atom. It was devised before that accurate picture could begin to be drawn. Yet, outmoded though it is, it is adequate for most purposes — and far, far more pleasing to the mind's eye than the atom's bewildering, smudgy reality.

These constructs are lifted from what some call, self-consciously, the "hard" sciences. Yet even these bastions of empirical rectitude display, as we have noted, an admiration for elegance of construct to cover gaps in concrete knowledge. The behavioral sciences, concerned as they are with the maddening and slippery complexities of body and mentality, have to make do with even more inference.

We administer an IQ test to a child. His score is lower than his classmates'. Since the IQ test is identical for all children who took the test, and the scores differ, we must presume that there is something going on inside the child that influences his ability to perform the specified tasks. We give this unknown intervening variable a label (intelligence) and presto! a construct is born. It is of course only a construct, only educated guesswork. We cannot see intelligence; we may only measure its ultimate effect. We cannot with all our surgical skill open the poor kid's skull and extract a "smart" suitable for slicing and microscopic analysis. But we are at least guardedly willing to allow that it exists (and argue bitterly about what it is).

Psychology deals with the scientific study of behavior. Organisms receive messages (stimuli) from the environment, and act (respond) in various ways to affect the environment in return (and sometimes respond involuntarily at the environment's command). All psychologists, more or less, agree with this general statement, this schema for behavior. At this critical point, however, the scientific study of behavior divides into three loosely bounded theoretical camps.

BEHAVIORISM

The most empirical set of theories (that is, the one which relies *least* on inferential variables or constructs and most on observed occurrences or data) is Behaviorism. In the strictest sense, what I shall call "hard-line Behaviorism" is not really a theory, but is actually atheoretical. This may sound harsh, but all it is meant to suggest is the fact that Behaviorism is really a hard-nosed set of investigative methods rather than theories. The Behaviorist approach is useful and rewarding if this limitation is kept in mind.

The fundamental idea of this school of thought is that human behavior can be adequately described by the simple relationship of stimulus and response (S-R psychology). All our behaviors are the result of triggering stimuli in the environment, now and in the past. Human mental activity and consciousness are nothing — or perhaps a "black box." The essence of behavior is ultimately reducible to S and R, like the popular image of the near-archetypal white rat daintily pressing the food bar in the operant conditioning chamber because such responses (R) are rewarded by appetitive stimuli (S^{R+}) which increase the probability that the bar-pressing response will recur. This whole subcreation of science is based on two laws: if something you do makes you happy, you will probably do it again; and the more you practice, the better you do it.

Other than the obvious emotional argument that humans are not rats (or, perhaps more accurately, that rats are not human) and the inescapable realization that Behaviorism and free will cannot exist together in the same universe, a significant body of the psychological discipline finds compelling reason to reject this approach as anything but investigative methodology. The argument is quite simple: people react in different ways to the same stimulus. Now this may be due to different learning experiences — that is, each individual will have had unique experiences with his environment and may consequently have learned to react in unique ways. But the strict behaviorists are firm: only S and R.

Of course what they *mean* is simply that the inferred processes inside the organism cannot be directly measured and are hence unworthy of scientific study. They exist, but are just too ethereal to bother with if your game is science.

These comments on Behaviorists are not really cheap shots. They are good people, by and large, and their excesses can be chalked up to prior learning. And, most important, we should remember that they entered psychology at a time of confusion, sweeping sloppy science and half-baked conventional wisdom out of the discipline like a reforming mayor in a wide-open town. The reader will, I hope, forgive me for saying that the reforming mayor gradually became dictatorial and intolerant, pushing those of more moderate persuasion into the periphery of the behavioral sciences for many years.

PSYCHODYNAMIC THEORIES

This general set of theories can be reconciled in some ways with Behaviorism. Imagine, if you will, a modification of the strict S-R way of looking at behavior; a modification which we call (after Woodworth) the S-O-R model. Stimulus and response are both there, but now we allow for the influence of *organismic* variables. These variables are given labels, and are in the nature of explanatory and predictive constructs. Intelligence is one of these. We present the IQ test (S) to the child (O — Organism), who produces a score (R). Since scores vary from subject to subject, we infer that some variable exists in the organism which mediates the nature of the response, and we give it a name: intelligence.

The psychodynamic theories embrace this modified Behaviorism* in a unique way. A man's behavior is the product of the dynamic interaction of internal organismic forces — the outcome of a battle of constructs. These "psychodynamics" result in the unique dimensions of personality.

Freud noted the occurrence of a variety of clinical symptoms that had no apparent medical cause, and gamely flew in the face of accepted medical wisdom by inferring a psychological rather than medical origin. He labeled these *psychoneuroses proper*. He eventually concluded that they were caused by strong influences in early childhood, chiefly the Oedipal situation, in which the child conceived a primitive physical sexual attraction for the parent of the opposite sex. Faulty mechanisms for dealing with this impossible situation at the time planted the seed for neurotic symptoms later in life. If we consider the complex S to be crisis in adulthood and the R to be neurotic symptoms, then we see Freud as faced with a sort of problem in conceptual algebra:

$$S(O) = R$$

or, "A given environmental situation, mediated by some unknown internal variable(s), yields certain characteristic responses which are symptomatic of mental disorder." Of course, solving for "O" is no pushover, but gradually Freud constructed a complex and internally consistent theoretical model. It was based on years of clinical observation, self-analysis, and therapy. It relied on a number of constructs.

The terms "conscious and unconscious" as theoretical mind "layers" represent pure inference derived from the ob-

---

* A calculated but misleading way to put it, since the earliest psychodynamic theorists predated the formal birth of Behaviorism as a coherent approach, and the S-O-R model was not presented until 1926, some years after Freud's *Psychopathology of Everyday Life*. I am artificially imposing the model to clarify a pretty abstruse concept.

servation that we are able to remember and introspect upon some things, bring them into awareness, but are unable to handle other memories and urges, which are for some reason unacceptable at a higher level of awareness. The dynamic of id-ego-superego is similarly composed of concepts invented for theoretical purposes; that is, they are merely constructs. Not even the most delicate surgery will yield a living ego. But, like the planetary atom, this framework allows us with our human conceptual limitations to visualize (if metaphorically) what Freud claimed to see bubbling and festering in the human mind. More important, it allows us to predict and explain within limits ideas and outcomes that would otherwise be incomprehensible.

The influence of Freud's theory has been so strong and pervasive that many of his most obscure concepts have come into wide abuse in everyday language. The term *ego* * has been stretched liberally in popular psychology to cover a variety of ideas that the original construct only vaguely subsumes in orthodox terminology. In the original sense, the ego is the controlling, protecting center of the personality, which arises from the infantile need to satisfy the demands of the innate, instinctual drives. These drives originate in an inborn repository of sexual motivation, which Freud called the id ("it"). The third partner in this psychological triumvirate is the superego. Most readers recognize this as the personification of social restraints — a conscience — but how many know that it arises, in the Freudian view, from the counter-cathexis of castration anxiety as it develops from the Oedipal lusts, and from the defensive identification with the loved and feared father? The byzantine interworkings of the Freudian mentality offer at the very least the most exhaustive explanation for human behavior.

* Literally "I" as in "me"; Freud, less inclined to Latinize, called it *das Ich*.

It is important to remember two basic articles of faith in Freudian theory: (1) Man is essentially hedonistic, motivated by the "pleasure principle"; even his most noble works may be no more than sublimated release of sexual energy in socially acceptable activity; and (2) Man's behavior is *determined* by his instinctive drives and the ways in which they are directed and apportioned in early childhood. In these respects, Freudian and Behaviorist are brothers under the skin. The pleasure principle is not wholly unlike the principle of reinforcement or Law of Effect: if a certain response results in satisfaction, it is likely to be repeated. Second, the idea of determinism is a least common denominator. All behaviors are learned; all responses result from triggering signals in the environment, hence all behavior is caused rather than initiated freely by the organism. The difference, of course, is in the willingness to employ internal variables to explain the behavior.

HUMANISM

Humanistic views of personality have gained in popularity in recent times as a collective genteel outrage over the ideas of hedonism and determinism. For one thing, the Freudian/Behaviorist view is rather pessimistic in its personification of Man, its basic view of human nature. Freud and Skinner might argue that "optimistic" and "pessimistic" are dimensionless terms — that human nature just happens, and that our evaluation of it is mere *post facto* critique. This is a rather breezy attitude, however, for those who reject the image of Man as a lust-crazed rat in the maze of existence, or a mere automaton responding blindly in a world full of demanding discriminative stimuli.

The Humanist movement, of course, predates Freud or the first controlled laboratory use of long-suffering *Rattus nor-*

veigicus. Humanism logically dates from the first conscious introspection of a hominid, his (for as that conscious thought occurred *it* became he*) first metaphorical attempt at self-definition. *Homo sapiens* is demonstrably the only species that teaches a course in general psychology. Mental activity is real, not just an after-the-fact effervescence, because we must have mental activity to conceive of mental activity. The strict Behaviorist might find this line of argument tautological, but at the same time consider the point not worth debating.

Essential to this series of theoretical perspectives (including existential analysis, phenomenology, constructive alternativism, and a host of peripheral theories that seem to possess the gestation and life span of a mayfly) are two common themes in direct opposition to Behaviorism and Freudian theory:

(1) *Motivation* is not solely the result of reinforcement or innate drives — we are being pulled upward to a final goal, not just pushed rudely by our past.

(2) Since not all behaviors are dictated by reinforcement or early toilet training or whatever, then the concept of *Free Will* can exist — we are to some extent captains of our souls.

The motivational construct of Humanism is generally one of fulfillment. Maslow and Rogers label this ultimate goal that leads us onward and upward self-actualization — the fulfillment of genetic potential. There is a basic plan for development of each of us, preprogrammed to some extent, and toward which we are inexorably drawn. This is a hard point to put across to undergraduate students, particularly cadets who have been conditioned (there — I said it!) to respond with structured solutions to problems. The analogy of the Chinese puzzle might be useful. The self is potentially spher-

* Or "he/she"; could an unconscious organism get upset about sexist psycholinguistics?

ical: imagine a perfect sphere with a magnetic field like the earth's, which is toroidal, shaped like a fat doughnut surrounding the sphere. This is the self in perfect balance. When we are born, this self does not exist, but as we mature, the self emerges in puzzle pieces from the background of the environment. If and when all the pieces fall together, the perfect sphere is formed, and the field is in balance; as long as pieces are missing or misplaced, the field is disturbed in potential. When we have assembled the puzzle ("put it all together"), we are self-actualized. Most of us never make it, but this does not reduce its attractive influence on our lives.

What is self-actualization like?

We are told that the self-actualized person is in close touch with himself, accepting his own peculiarities with little difficulty, and at the same time accepting others without distorted judgment. His concept of reality is less refracted by selfish personal needs; he has less inclination to twist or rationalize experience to fit a demanding and jealous self-concept. He is concerned with global issues, the fate of Man. By definition, however, he is not a "perfect" person. He can be crabby, shallow, and ruthless because of his strength and self-reliance.

This idea is echoed in the existentialist's concept of "being-in-the-world" (*Dasein*) and in George Kelly's hard-nosed theories about perfecting personal constructs. But there is another common feature of these theories, which binds them together and which will begin to have relevance when we begin to probe the hobbit psyche. That is the idea of *incongruence* or *alienation* or deviation from core role constructs.

Imagine that we are on a preordained path (as toward self-actualization), according to healthy growth patterns. No personality may exist in a vacuum; there are competing drives, not only physiological and social needs, but the norms and collective demands of others, of society. Carl Rogers notes our need for positive regard — "good vibes" — from others, the need for respect, liking, approval. Others may attach conditional restrictions to this gift ("I will love you *if* you [clean your room] [obey orders] [get a promotion] [bring home a good report card] [be nice to your little brother] [stop pounding away at that stupid typewriter and take me out once in a while]," etc.). This leads us on a course away from that one which will finally lead to fulfillment. The gap, which Rogerians call incongruence, the existentialists alienation, is really no more than the distance between where we are and where we should be. The greater the gap, the greater the sense of unease. The tired housewife who thinks wistfully of the lost promise of a career knows this feeling. The insurance salesman who retires from the trade and sits before the typewriter waiting for the novel to spring forth and finds only emptiness knows it. Many of my colleagues — often the most promising soldiers, men I served with in the frustration of training and the boredom and brief exhilarating terror of combat — sensed that awful chasm in their early thirties, the threatening awareness that they had somehow become fictitious people. They came to see their beliefs as imposed by others, by transient group impulse and tradition, felt that they were treading the wrong path, and sadly they resigned.

My students discover, usually dismayingly late in the semester, that these theories are more alike in some ways than different. The reason for this is quite plain: no matter who is doing the observing and theorizing, the behaviors from which theories are abstracted are by and large consistent, and the nominally competitive theories are necessarily elaborations of the same theme. But some of the differences are real. There is a great deal of unanimity on the subject of gravity. This is not unexpected. I can drop the eraser a thousand times in class and it will fall *down* every time (at least it always has). On the other hand, I have never been able to predict what my children will do in any given situation — at

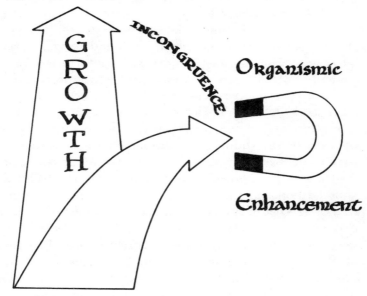

FIGURE 1. THE CONCEPT OF INCONGRUENCE

least not as confidently as I predict the eraser's path. There are too many intervening variables in human behavior, and any attempt to dissect them and sketch their boundaries and functions is a perilous quest, and no less filled with dark tunnels, frightening rumors, and fantastic discoveries than the road to the Cracks of Doom.

Tolkien's vast map of Middle-earth and its dizzying array of strange beasts, rich history, enchanting landscape, and the rhythmic prose and poetry of the quest itself, is no more or less than an intricate map of the human psyche; as in fact all forms of human expression are ultimately drawn from that inexhaustibly creative source. Reality, such as it exists in the individual sense, is formed, refracted, and tinted by the subjective dynamics of mentality.

Tolkien's map is not without theoretical usefulness. The pervasive influence of certain themes and images described by Jung's theory of personality shape the form and symbolic content of Middle-earth, for each reader to appreciate according to his unique personal needs. I have chosen the Jungian framework because Tokien's work is probably the clearest repository of Jungian themes in recent literature. Whether the creator of Middle-earth employed these shapes of the psyche deliberately or not is a matter of debate, and the reader will draw his own conclusions. Despite Tolkien's devout Catholicism and concern with Christian theology, *The Lord of the Rings* is no more constrained by Christian theology than is the *Poetic Edda*. Archetype is more powerful than allegory, as Professor Tolkien was clearly aware. The strength of those powerful common symbols is measured by the number of people willing, in this jaded age, to lay down the price of a three-volume book of "fantasy." The answer is not in fantasy at all, despite our mundane interpretations — no more fantasy than the *Book of the Dead* to an ailing Pharaoh!

But Jung's theory is most complex, and few readers will have much familiarity with its mechanisms — nor, happy to say, the misconceptions that still unfairly plague Freud's reputation among the untutored. I have tried in these few pages to sketch in the broader outlines of personality theory. Now it remains to place Jung's theoretical stance in its proper position and introduce the reader to this new set of constructs, an organized and engrossing view of what we are, how we got that way, and what will become of us.

II
theory and construct
in analytical psychology

CARL G. JUNG occupies a pivotal position in the hierarchy of personality theorists. His intricate system of theoretical constructs is undeniably psychodynamic, no less so than Freud's. Yet his insistence upon the realization of the Self as the ultimate goal of the psyche foreshadows the more widely known concept of self-actualization.* The usual gauge of power in a personality theory is its relative popularity as a therapeutic strategy — that is, the acceptance of the theory in a clinical sense as a method of treatment. In this sense, Jung has never enjoyed wide popularity in the United States, but rather has maintained a modest number of loyal adherents.

In the broader sense, however, Jungian ideas have had widespread impact; and this is, paradoxically, part of the reason for his equivocal status in American psychology. It

---

* A point that more than one writer has been quick to note, though the Humanists seldom cite Jung as a source — possibly because of a self-conscious reluctance to anchor their theoretical structures to a psychodynamic theorist. Some analytical writers credit Jung, nevertheless, as the first self-actualization theorist.

takes guts, real iron-clad viscera, to be eclectic and interdisciplinary in psychology. Psychology is a body of knowledge and speculation with, you will forgive the expression, a sensitive ego. Until quite recently psychology was more or less the scientific cutting edge of philosophy and the soft trailing edge of a variety of other academic disciplines. As late as the nineteenth century (with a few holdouts even today) medicine disavowed any connection with psychology, equating that study with mesmerism and other quackery, much as engineering and mathematics instructors at West Point lump the most rigorous psychophysicist or rat-runner together with practitioners of exorcism, permissiveness, free sex, and other "touchie-teelie" pursuits. You begin to see the sort of problems Freud faced as a doctor of medicine who pioneered in psychological models of disorder. As we have seen, there is even now a schism between those who accept only empirical data and those who are sporting enough to take a chance on conceptual models to explain and predict when the demonstrative approach is impossible. The former camp is sensitive to any ideas that smell even faintly of magic. Psychology is, like all new and growing disciplines, intensely jealous of the boundaries of its intellectual domain.

As a consequence, theorists who use evidence from sources other than the laboratory or the consulting room are occasionally regarded askance. Jung borrowed from religion, history, art, mythology, literature, and a host of related fields of human endeavor to shape and support his ideas. This investigative approach stood to reason, in the philosophical sense that all forms of human expression spring ultimately from the human mind and so ultimately provide clues to the nature of the unknown machinations therein (which is all Jung was saying); but in the popular view of the fledgling behavioral sciences inference of this sort — particularly inference based on other, comparatively nonscientific fields — had the aura of anathema if not outright heresy. That this reaction is one of self-consciousness rather than true intellectual rigor is suggested by the ease with which more established scientific disciplines accept concepts like the planetary atom and the wave and particle models of light without blushing. We psychologists feel threatened by a shadow, so to speak — the "shadow" of our philosophical (to say nothing of magical) past.

Carl Gustav Jung was born in Kesswil, Switzerland, in 1875. He died in 1961. He wrote and speculated through much of his life and published a great volume of these reflections. Like Freud, his impact on psychology was assured: anyone who speculates that long and writes that much is bound to influence *somebody*. This is particularly true when you are in an age of pioneers in your field, as were Freud and Jung. In these times it almost seems that anyone with an electric typewriter can be a great oracle of human behavior, if only for a brief season.

Jung's father was a Protestant pastor, and his interest in religion dates from an early age. But even in its formative stages, his concept of God was unusually creative, evoking both wonder and fear in his childhood. His interests were, however, far too broad and far-reaching, his intellectual curiosity too intense, to tolerate the narrow confines of Swiss Calvinism. He recognized in his childhood concepts of religion — unconventional though they were in the strict sense — the essence of primitive ritual. These curious ideas of childhood and his later sensitivity to common themes in human behavior and expression led him to conclude that certain aspects of the mind are common to all men. This fairly early observation led ultimately to his life's obsession.

Despite his diffuse interests he harbored a desire to better the lot of humanity, and chose as his profession the practice of medicine. He studied psychiatry (which meant the medical, not psychological, investigation and treatment of mental disorder — the idea of psychological models being still in infancy), and practiced under the famous Dr. Eugen Bleuler at the mental hospital at Burgholzli. His chief interest was the severe mental disorder dementia praecox, which Bleuler had recently renamed the "group of schizophrenias."

Jung was intrigued, then fascinated by the published work of Freud, which was by then beginning to appear in journals. The investigations and breakthroughs in dream analysis particularly caused him to reflect on his youthful preoccupations, and he found many of Freud's observations and clinical experiences useful in gaining insights in the thought patterns of schizophrenic patients. In his comments on Freud's death in 1939, Jung credited Freud's work as "probably the boldest attempt that has ever been made to master the riddles of the unconscious psyche upon the apparently firm ground of empiricism. For us, then young psychiatrists, it was . . . a source of illumination, while for our older colleagues it was an object of mockery."[1]

They were a beleaguered band of brothers in the early days, these psychoanalysts. Often attacked by a righteous public, reviled and isolated by their medical colleagues, hard put to find willing printers, they stubbornly persisted in the battle to win legitimacy for their techniques. Freud was the acknowledged patriarch of the Viennese analysts, and exercised considerable moral suasion for several years over Jung and his Zurich associates. But success came, and it ultimately spoiled the unanimity of the psychoanalytic discipline. First Adler rejected Freud's fatherly domination, then Jung led the Swiss delegation away from the fold. The latter split was especially traumatic for Freud, who had

[1] Jung, *Memories, Dreams, Reflections*, p. 169 ff.

regarded Jung as a trusted disciple. Jung was not prepared to be anyone's disciple, however, and the split was aggravated by certain doctrinal problems in orthodox psychoanalysis that he found unacceptable.

The major point of disagreement was the matter of Freud's overwhelming emphasis on sexuality as the universal motivator. "Here," Jung reports, "I could not agree with Freud. He considered the cause of repression to be sexual trauma. From my practice, however, I was familiar with several cases of neurosis in which . . . sexuality played a subordinate part."[2] Jung never broke entirely (at least in his own view) with Freud; the older psychoanalyst was unable nevertheless to tolerate heresy, and the close personal bond between them dissolved with some acrimony. Certain aspects of Freudian theory were retained by Jung, and this is a factor often overlooked in assessments of the latter's work.

But this book is not intended to be a biography of Jung, nor a history of psychoanalysis. It now remains to provide a picture of Jung's own theoretical framework. It cannot be much more than a superficial sketch, which I promise to elaborate later whenever the concepts apply to Tolkien's work. Jung's concept of the psyche is not easy to visualize, being more complex and subtle than Freud's. For greater clarity, I have added at strategic points some graphic representations — but I must add the caution that *any* visualization is just that, a simplistic rendering which only approximates artificially something that cannot be accurately drawn.

In the beginning, the psyche was no more a conscious human gadget than the nervous responses of a cockroach or a rat — stimulus-bound, unconscious, responding more or less robotlike to its environmental cues. The psyche evolved as the

[2] Ibid., p. 170.

human brain and the human form evolved, part of the gradual adaptation of the species from the primordial past to the emergence of *Man* as an organism dramatically different from what had come before. This evolution was clearly based on incremental changes in the electrochemical structures of the brain, but these processes are so little understood that we might as well consider them metaphysical; the explanations of mental activity as a function of neurological activity will emerge as research methods improve, but in the meantime we must satisfy ourselves with roundabout metaphors.

This dividing line between Man and pre-Man was the emergence of consciousness, though the unconscious remains as a substrate. The differentiation of conscious and unconscious is in principle the same as Freud's statement. The conscious is an outward-looking expression of the personality, what we are thinking about now plus what we can think about as we wish. The unconscious includes our evolutionary underpinnings — the "animal" part of us, which is a sometimes embarrassing vestige of phylogenetic heritage — and certain ideas and feelings which are kept *out* of consciousness.

FIGURE 2. GENERAL MODEL OF THE PSYCHE

It may help to visualize Jung's concept of the psyche as the *circular hyperboloid* on the facing page. In general, upward direction leads to the conscious, downward toward the unconscious. Direction of energy upward is "outward-looking"; I will use Jung's term *extraversion* to denote this. Direction of energy downward (which is obviously also *inward*) I will call *introversion*. The narrowest part of the hyperboloid represents the permeable boundary between conscious and unconscious. The outer end, the social environment, is dominated by a collective consciousness, managed (as we shall see) by conscious forces; the inner world is influenced by the collective unconscious, which we may think of as an evolutionary environment. It is not an "environment" in the objective sense, because the "inputs" are not really from outside the organism; they are innate *within* the organism. But if we bother to separate personal and collective unconsciousness, then it is not illogical to think of the personal part as figure on the ground of the collective experience. The arrows represent the potential for exchange between the two realms.

collective · conscious
social · environment·

outward·looking·
[extroverted]

unconscious   conscious

[introverted]
·inward·looking

evolutionary· environment·
·collective· unconscious

Jung hinted that this differentiation was reflected in the Greek myth of Prometheus. Consciousness is the twofold gift: fire (cleverness, technology, and mastery over nature) and the power to foresee death (introspection and a sense of Self). In a sense, these gifts have made us godlike — and the gods have never forgiven us or Prometheus![3]

Jung calls these divisions of the psyche the *personal conscious* and *personal unconscious*, but these do not tell the whole story. His recognition of the recurrences of the theme in myth, art, dreams, religion, and the broadest areas of human expression — similarities which are cross-cultural — suggest the presence of promptings that are common to all men. He called these primordial images, or *archetypes*. These are inborn predispositions, the collective experience of race and species. Jung uses the metaphor of the stream bed:

> Archetypes resemble the beds of rivers: dried up because the water has deserted them, though it may return at any time. An archetype is something like an old watercourse along which the water of life has flowed for a time, digging a deep channel for itself. The longer it flowed the deeper the channel, and the more likely it is that sooner or later the water will return.[4]

The flow of consciousness, like the water, not only shapes the stream bed, but is channeled by it. The repeated common experiences of the psyche are engraved by generations of use. All humans have mothers. This collective experience yields the mother archetype, a predisposed mother image, which is projected onto the real mother after birth, and by abstraction becomes the Earth Mother, Blessed Virgin, and a host of related symbolic renderings. The rising and setting of

---

[3] Jung, *Two Essays on Analytical Psychology*, p. 154 f.
[4] Jung, "Wotan", in *Civilization in Transition*, p. 12.

sun and moon, the experience of light and darkness, ages of social contact with others of the species — all these contribute to the formation of the archetypes. These images form the basis for what Jung labeled the *collective unconscious*, the repository of phylogenetic experience. These archetypes do not reveal themselves directly, as we shall see, but through *symbols*, which emerge into consciousness.

A conscious archetype is the *ego* or *ego complex*.* This construct is similar to Freud's ego, in that it is the directing force. However, the ego in the Jungian sense is an imperfect controlling agent because it is based in the conscious realm and responds to conscious needs only. It directs behaviors not only according to internal promptings, but also according to the expectations and restraints of social pressure. It does this through the *persona*, a social façade, which meets the expectations (or what we choose to consider the expectations) of others. It has been described as a *collective conscious*,[5] which is true enough in a sense, but perhaps unfairly suggests an opposition to the collective unconscious. The most logical balance of the latter is the objective environment, the world outside the psyche — or at least our present phenomenal† experience of it — just as the collective unconscious might be called a subjective environment to the extent that it reflects the individual record of past environments even to remote antiquity; an experiential "stew" of which one's Self is only an ingredient. The persona, in any case, is the mask we as-

* The term *complex* refers to the tendency of ideas and feelings to coalesce into more complex structures, hence the choice of the label.
[5] Rychlak, *Introduction to Personality and Psychotherapy*, p. 138.
† The term *phenomenal* is applied in psychology to the concept of individual subjective experience of the world, rather than objective experience. Our view of the world is tinted by the limitations of our perceptual abilities and the influence of internal variables. Phenomenology is an essential part of most existential-Humanistic theories of personality.

sume to make the outward-looking manifestations of the psyche fit the assigned social roles and expectations.

The name persona is drawn from the Greek mask of classical drama, and the analogy is very appropriate. The persona might be compared to the concept of a need for positive regard suggested by the later theorist Carl Rogers — this need is personified by Jung as the cluster of behaviors which the ego manipulates to gain social approval. We literally don the mask to play our social roles.

Two ideas are central to the importance of the persona. It is intimately connected with the ego, and in fact the ego may come to identify with the persona (there is no longer a clear contrast between the inner personality and the social personality), a case in which it is not clear which archetype is manipulating which, and we stop being content to fool others and begin earnestly fooling ourselves. Second, the persona is a necessary part of the personality despite its troublesome aspects, since the origins of the persona are archetypal, part of the ontogenetic blueprint for development. It is not maintained without risk, however — an overemphasis of consciousness, the ego-persona activities, causes the very problem which the Ringbearer, like any ordinary person faced with life, must seek to resolve.

Despite our modern emphasis on the conscious, our animal ancestry remains a potent force in our lives. The "animal" or lower, base, instincts are relegated by the ego into the depths of the unconscious. The core of this complex is the archetypal remnant of evolution from lower forms. Around this nucleus a complex of ideas and emotions begins to cluster, bits of material inconsistent with the persona's proud mask. Jung called this complex the *shadow* or alter-ego, and it is no less than the personification of the dark side of man's nature, the beastly phylogenetic heritage.

Jung reported a dream that gave the name and form to this potent archetype:

> It was night in some unknown place, and I was making slow and painful headway against a mighty wind. Dense fog was flying along everywhere. I had my hands cupped around a tiny light which threatened to go out at any moment. Everything depended on my keeping this little light alive. Suddenly I had the feeling that something was coming up behind me. I looked back and saw a gigantic black figure following me. But at the same moment I was conscious, in spite of my terror, that I must keep my little light going through night and wind, regardless of all dangers.[6]

Jung awoke with the realization that the dark follower was nothing more than his own shadow cast on the mist by the flickering candle.

This has always reminded me of Coleridge's traveler in *The Rime of the Ancient Mariner* who looks back on the road, then "no more turns his head/because he knows a frightful fiend doth close behind him tread." It is clear at least from Jung's dream that this figure is no "frightful fiend" but the "spectre of the Brocken," a figure that appears only by grace of the light cast by the tiny candle. The candle is the flickering, uncertain light of consciousness; the spectral shadow is the other self, the vestige of Man's evolution, the dark side of his nature. The weakness of modern Man is his personification of the shadow of his own nature as a frightful fiend, and the unwillingness to turn his head.

Akin to but distinct from the shadow is the archetype of bisexuality. The physiological ambiguity of Man has long

[6] Jung, *Memories, Dreams, Reflections*, pp. 107–8.

- social environment -
collective conscious

ego

self

shadow

- ar(ch)ecy(p)es -
collective unconscious
evolutionary substrate

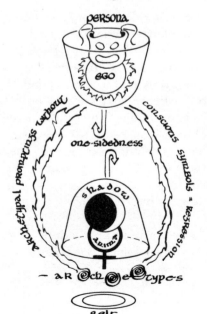

persona

ego

archetypal promptings without   conscious symbols = regression

one-sidedness

shadow

anima

- ar(ch)(e)types -

self

been accepted — not only in physical form, which we can easily verify in a full-length mirror, but in the simple fact that both male and female hormones are present in both sexes. This physiological vestige, combined with generations of racial experience with the opposite sex, gives rise to a complex of ideas and emotions that is identified by cultural standards as unacceptable other-sex characteristics. Sentiment, emotionality, empathy, disclosure — these dimensions have long been identified, at least in our own culture, with female attributes.* The female psyche is likewise graced with an other-sex, *macho* sort of complex composed of repressed nominally male roles and feelings. Jung calls these archetypes the *anima* (in men) and *animus* (in women).

The ego rules the personality's conscious face, and the shadow and anima hold sway in the unconscious, but buried in the collective unconscious is the possibility of a new con-

* I recall vividly the sight of Vietnamese men holding hands in friendship, a gesture of familiarity which carried no cultural stigma, when I was a young officer overseas for the first time. I was scandalized.

FIGURE 3. PSYCHIC DYNAMICS AND EGO-CONSCIOUSNESS

The drawing at the top is an elaboration of the general model in Figure 2; it represents the *idealized* function of the psyche. The ego, symbolized by the sun, dominates consciousness; unconscious function is centered around the shadow, symbolized by the moon. The Self is at the midpoint of the psyche, and serves as the channel for creative exchange between the two realms. The archetypes of the collective unconscious are represented by spirals; their contributions are passed into conscious symbolization by the Self, the connecting link.

The drawing on the bottom represents the typical psyche dominated by one-sidedness. The hyperboloid has given way to two separate paraboloids, suggesting the estrangement of conscious and unconscious processes. The persona (shown in the form of its namesake mask) imposes outward conscious behaviors, the anima "stands behind" and manipulates the shadow. The Self is only a potential force buried in the collective unconscious.

The flaming trail represents the inability of unconscious creative forces (in the form of libido) to find symbolization in the conscious; the "homeless" libido *regresses* into the unconscious.

trolling force: the *Self.* * This archetype has the inherent potential to replace the ego as the new center of personality, a healthy force which can bind together the conscious and its unconscious substrate. The search for the Self is the final goal of the psyche, and the theme of *The Lord of the Rings*.

The problem is, of course, that we cannot safely deny our unconscious instinctive underpinnings. The shadow and anima are necessary integral parts of the totality of the psyche, and can only be ignored at grave risk. Here we must plunge briefly into a construct system which is considerably harder to grasp, since it relies upon analogy from physics. An understanding of human motivation is central to the problem of the Ring, however, so here it is:

Freud had theorized that human behavior is *powered* by a construct energy which he called *libido.* † This was the sex drive, the instinctive orientation toward all things that lead to physical satisfaction. Jung retained the basic concept of a psychic energy, including the name libido, but to him it was a life drive rather than a sex drive. Libido provides the impetus for all thoughts and intentions, and it operates on the principle of opposites. For every "good" thought there is a corresponding "bad" one. The former may be expressed consciously, the latter triggering an opposite reaction in the unconscious that is repressed; there it may form part of the greater shadow complex. The mere fact that it is dumped into this dimly lit psychic dustbin does not mean that the energy is dissipated, the problem being not unlike disposal of nuclear waste; quite the contrary, a situation of disequilibrium occurs, the phenomenon of *one-sidedness.* This means

---

* Actually, since it has not at this point been realized, it is more properly called the Self-in-potentia.

† To be perfectly correct, *libido* refers to the energy associated with eros, the life instinct. *Thanatos*, the death instinct, was fueled by a force Freud never presumed to name.

simply that the libido is obedient to the First Law of Thermodynamics: energy is neither created nor destroyed. The psyche must also come to grips with the Second Law, the law of entropy: systems tend to equilibrium, to the simplest possible form. This implies that one-sidedness is like an electrical potential, an imbalance which creates of itself a need for equilibrium.

Bear in mind that the libido potential cannot be measured with a galvanometer. The idea is a construct, in this case a borrowed analogy of convenience from the physical sciences, which Jung uses, *not because it is real and measurable* in the absolute sense, but because it allows us to visualize what is beyond us to comprehend otherwise. A simple rule in theory is to keep the constructs that fit (as this one does) and throw out the rest — and keep trying to build testable hypotheses!

Archetypes in themselves contain "stored libido," which Jung calls *numen*. The larger complexes are charged this way, and may inherit energy by virtue of one-sidedness. This is because they are repressed into the unconscious by the ego and thus have no opportunity to "express themselves" and so relieve the buildup of energy. To be realized in the conscious, appropriate symbols must be available. These symbols may emerge in dreams, religious expression, art, mythology, fiction, or any of a host of channels. The unavailability of these channels may aggravate the formation of one-sidedness.

One-sidedness is the foundation of neurotic disturbance in Jungian practice, as the unresolved Oedipal conflict served as the source of disorder in Freudian theory. This denial of the total psyche, the repudiation of the essential contribution of the unconscious, is derived from two sources: the dominance of the ego in its efforts to maintain the persona, which requires the repression of thoughts and urges inconsistent with the public mask; and the unavailability of conscious symbols through which the archetypal forces may be expressed and the imbalance relieved. In symptom, one-sidedness may begin as a feeling of nothingness, boredom, malaise, not unlike the "alienation" of existential neurosis or alternatively in a variety of other common symptoms of distress. To the extent that the persona is a conscious fiction, the ego has become a conscious fiction that tyrannically thrusts away the promptings of the whole psyche in favor of the conventional restraints of society.

It may seem puzzling that the key to wholeness is the acceptance of essentially "evil" impulses of the shadow. But the shadow is not necessarily evil, merely less sophisticated; and in any case is part of the whole picture. Duality is an essential part of all human perceptions. Good can exist philosophically only as a figure against a ground of evil, and vice versa. Light is a figure on a ground of darkness, never against a background of nothing, for nothing cannot really be conceived or visualized. In *The Two Hands of God* Alan Watts suggests that:

> There is a point, not at all easy to determine, at which inattention and opposition to the essential ambivalence of nature becomes neurotic . . . For the dark side of life, the principle of evil or of man's irreducible rascality, is to be "reckoned with . . ."[7]

This one-sidedness may to some extent be culturally shared. Jung points out that the dwindling of religious expression in the West (coupled with the pursuit of conscious materialism) has left a gap in the psychic functioning which is common to many individual lives.[8] When the symbols that

---

[7] Alan W. Watts, *The Two Hands of God*, p. 24.
[8] Jung, *Psychology and Alchemy*, p. 9.

once promoted wholeness by allowing expression of unconscious needs are removed or allowed to wither, trouble invariably results. The outcome may be a loss of purpose or
evasive tactics, expression of urges in other, sometimes vio-
lent, ways. The American Plains Indian culture, deprived of
its gods and values and repaid with Protestant missions, hun-
ger, and whiskey, yielded to the bottle or the millennialist
Ghost Dance movement. The Kikuyu of Kenya, having
abandoned their ages-old spiritual values, exploded in the
terrible Mau Mau revolt. The search for the soul may be vio-
lent or pathetic. The long enslavement of poverty, spiritual
and economic, of the poor Jamaican blacks gave rise finally to
the desperate Rastafarian movement, with its touching deification of the late Emperor Haile Selassie. There is more to
the Rasta Man than reggae; he is the model for any society
that has been cruelly split off from its access to deeper
promptings, then tries devoutly to win them back.

What are the other archetypes?

Jung discovered a number of primordial images after years
of search and analysis. The common experiences — mother,
father, family, child — are so repetitive that they have
formed inherent predisposing structures in the brain. Hero,
hostile brethren, animals in human form and gods in animal
form, are sufficiently cross-cultural to have achieved archetypal status.

Archetypes are divided in form and function into *personifying* and *transforming* varieties (roughly analogous to noun and
verb). The personifying archetypes generally take human or
anthropomorphic form, and are expressed symbolically as
human or humanlike figures. Transforming archetypes are
nonpersonal situations and forms (quaternity, order, mandala, etc.) that have significance in psychic development.
When an archetype abandons its mute potential forces and
plays a significant part in conscious functioning, it is said to

be (a) dominant. Archetypal symbols may appear as guides provided by the unconscious to lead the psyche toward transformation. Some important archetypes (such as the Self) may be either personifying or transforming, representing either the path to Self-realization or personifying the finished product.

Since we will be intimately concerned with the archetype of the Self and its appearance in cultural forms, it is worth closer investigation. In its personifying form, the Self may appear as male, female, or (more particularly) a union of the two as opposites which together make up the whole (i.e., hermaphroditic). Christ is a figure that combines opposites (God + Man, spiritual + corporeal), and hence represents aspects of the Self. Since the Self represents the potential unity and balance of the psyche, it may also appear as a symmetrically balanced image with transformational qualities. The *mandala* or wheel of life may perform this symbolic transforming function. It is in form a symmetrical squared circle; the name *mandala* refers to the complex variety of designs of this type (mantras) common in Hindu and Tantric Buddhist art. The eightfold path of Buddhism is often represented in this way: an eight-spoked wheel (each spoke representing one aspect of the path to enlightenment), with the yin-yang, the Taoist union of opposites, in the center. The Celtic cross follows this theme, the cross of Christianity intersected by a coronal circle — a symbol with its roots in paganism and its branches in medieval faith. The swastika provides both symmetry and dynamic motion and is, as the world learned to its dismay, evocative of powerful emotions. Interestingly, Tolkien used elaborate mandala forms as artistic motifs in his own paintings and illustrations (as did Jung). One boxed paperback edition of his work is decorated with them, a decorative theme that may puzzle browsers in book stores, but which would be less trivial to an analytical psychologist!

swastika

yin-yang

celtic cross

eightfold path

FIGURE 4. ARTISTIC REPRESENTATIONS OF THE SELF

The yin-yang design, an oriental symbol widely known in the West (it appears in the center of the flag of the Republic of Korea), symbolizes the Self as an explicit union of opposites. It reminds us that there are two sides to any form, including the psyche. The yang is analogous to the feminine: the *hun* principle, lower, earthbound; the yin is the masculine: *p'o*, the higher, breath, soul.[9]

Related to the mandala is the idea of *quaternity*, the symbolic occurrence of things in fours or multiples of four. This is often merged with the mandala (note the eightfold path and Celtic cross in Figure 4). Although the triangle is more stable than the square in a structural sense (as you will know if you have ever challenged an Erector Set or built a garage), the three-sided form is psychically incomplete, denoting not balance but polarity, power, and movement.[10] But every up must have a down, every right a left. A three-sided figure is troublesomely asymmetrical; the psyche is always waiting for the fourth side to appear. This assertion of the Self finds symbolization in a variety of human endeavors. The ancient city of Babylon was arranged in rough mandala form, with four gates oriented in the cardinal directions, each dedicated to a major god.* Romanesque churches (and Roman military camps) were laid out on this general form. I have wondered whether our military troubles since World War II stem from headquartering the Department of Defense in a five-sided building.

Jung takes the Council of Nicaea firmly to task for the concept of the Trinity. He pointed out that the triune deity is so unbalanced that Satan or the Antichrist was attached with

---

[9] Jung, "Commentary on the Secret of the Golden Flower" in *Alchemical Studies*, pp. 38–39.

[10] Jung, *The Archetypes and the Collective Unconscious*, pp. 234–35.

* And the ordinal directions to demons. Of these archetypal beauties only Pazuzu, personification of the southeast and the plague wind and star of *The Exorcist*, is widely remembered. In the modern novel and motion picture, he appears as the personified animus of his host.

studied informality to fill the gap; then, centuries after the dark side of God became hard to handle theologically, a Papal Bull (*Munificentessimus Deus*) formalized the assumption and deification of the Virgin Mary and tentatively completed the "quaternalizing" of an uncomfortable godhead. Jung also implies that Protestantism remained archetypally behind in the race for the realization of the religious Self.[11]

It is important to remind ourselves at this point of the importance of teleology, or goal-direction, in contrast to Freud's gloomy presumptions of determinism. Our motivation is directed toward the ultimate joining of conscious and unconscious, and to the emergence of the Self as the new center of a balanced psyche. This is the final achievement to which these archetypal urges direct us. The Trickster in fairy tales may provide us with elusive clues; the Wise Old Man, archetype of wisdom and power, may guide us; the redeemer may sacrifice himself for the quest. Without the final goal of Self-realization, the symbols are only curiosities.

Our repertoire of symbols is dizzying in its variety and brilliance — Tolkien created and peopled a world with them through the fountainhead of his imagination, then brought them to their conclusion in the moment of triumphal union.

The process by which the Self is realized in life is called *individuation*. The first step toward this goal is no more than the realization of an unconscious element, glancing over our shoulders and perceiving the "frightful fiend." This is not a comforting experience. The shadow is the alter ego, the unconscious counterpart of the accustomed conscious personality. To ensure Self-realization — to pave the way for the Self, really — the unconscious complex must be accepted, not stifled and repressed. Note that the objective is not the destruction of the shadow, but rather its recognition, since the shadow is a necessary part of the whole. Nor does the shadow replace the ego, for this would be just as one-sided as

[11] Franz, *C. G. Jung: His Myth in Our Time*, pp. 191–92.

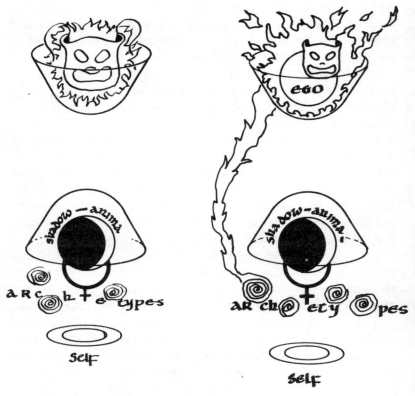

FIGURE 5. INFLATION

This illustration simplifies the idea of inflation. In the drawing on the left, the ego has identified with its persona; the two share libido, resulting in figurative expansion of the consciousness.

On the right, the ego has identified with an archetype. The result is the same — the field of libido is increased, and the conscious functions are subjected to bizarre expansion of apparent power.

the original arrangement (and probably rather unpleasant for those who would have to deal with such a beauty).*

But the ego need not confront the shadow directly, in single combat. Standing behind the shadow is the anima, the repressed other-sex complex. I prefer to think of the anima as balancing the shadow and compensating to a degree its sinister aspects. The anima or animus may be viewed as a contrasexual psyche, and in some ways the source of inspiration from the unconscious. The process of individuation requires the emergence of the anima as a conscious personification, since persons may be more easily dealt with than things. Confrontation with archetypal figures serves two purposes: it reduces their powerful intrusions into consciousness (dreams, etc.) without repressing them still more forcefully and thus worsening the problem, and it makes their stored libido available for healthy activities on both sides of the conscious-unconscious border. This allows the compensating elements of the psyche to join in wholeness, linked by the transcendental function of the Self. The anima and the façade of the persona are thus made less powerful, allowing the ego and shadow to coexist as representatives of their respective realms. The Self has emerged ("been realized") as the new midpoint of an integrated personality, the pathway from light to darkness. The psyche is united and balanced, one-sidedness finally resolved.

This has been a necessarily concise description of a set of concepts that fills many volumes. I will expand on these comments as needed in dealing with the specific issues of Middle-earth, but it is vital that we bear in mind this general process of Self-realization, now that we are ready to examine the significance of the War of the Ring.

---

* Of course, the ego need not be "good" in the objective social sense, nor the shadow "bad". Antisocial personalities may repress good impulses that would coalesce into a socially adaptive shadow.

anima personified in conscious.

shadow

arctype⊙pes

self

FIGURE 6. INDIVIDUATION

Note that the anima has moved into the conscious as a personified force which may confront the ego. This dynamic allows the built-up energy of the anima to be dissipated by "depotentiation," an antidote to one-sidedness.

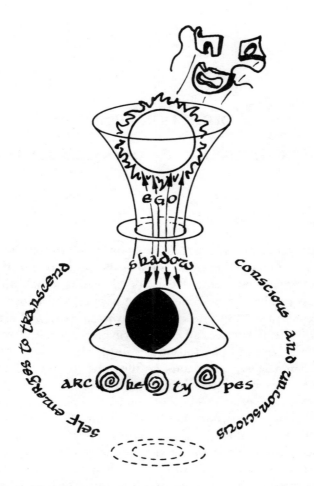

FIGURE 7. THE TRANSCENDENTAL FUNCTION AND THE HEALTHY PSYCHE

The anima has been depotentiated, and the persona is no longer a powerful force (its original existence was prompted to a large extent by the need to repress material inconsistent with the social environment); its unconscious counterpart has been tamed. The Self emerges from the collective unconscious to the midpoint of the personality as a new central controlling function; both ego and shadow remain, but neither dominates. The psyche is balanced.

III

númenor lost:

the neurosis of middle-earth

THE INFORMED SPECULATIONS of modern astrophysics
suggest a universe that burst forth at the beginning of time in
a blinding thermonuclear flash, the "big bang" that still survives as a pale luminescence encompassing the edges of an
ever-expanding totality of matter. From this original creative
tumult came all matter, all energy, rushing ever outward in a
swelling sphere of light and power until, almost as if foretold
by a cosmic seeress, the stars go out, one by one, in ages of
twilight followed by eternal darkness.

By coincidence, the view of modern Man, based on the
physical sciences, is not too different from that of the prime-
val metaphysics of earlier times. This is no less than the image
of God, no less than the image of the psyche, the ancient
projection of the human soul's self-image onto the universe
that surrounds him. The psychologist Marie-Louise von
Franz recounts and interprets the neoplatonic philosopher
Plotinus' elegant model:

> The center of being is the One,* the Light which radiates
> in all directions and into the infinite; this One is sur-

* Tolkien used the same expression (Eru) to describe his fictional divinity; I
do not mean to suggest that the relationship of the creation-images of the

rounded by the spherical covering of the world soul and, further out, by the visible cosmos. But the center is the "spiritual sphere" . . . which is unity, wholeness and the godhead itself.[1]

Fourteen centuries later, John Milton addressed this same moment of divine creation, the primordial vision:

> *"Let there be Light!" said God; and forthwith Light*
> *Ethereal, first of things, quintessence pure,*
> *Sprung from the Deep, and from her native East*
> *To journey in the airy gloom began,*
> *Sphered in radiant cloud — for yet the sun*
> *Was not; she in a cloudy tabernacle*
> *Sojourned the while. God saw the Light was good;*
>
> . . . .
>
> *By the celestial choirs, when orient light*
> *Exhaling first from darkness they beheld,*
> *Birth-day of Heaven and Earth. With joy and shout*
> *The hollow universal orb they filled.*[2]

At its beginning, Tolkien's world is scarcely distinguishable from the image shared by Plotinus and Milton. The Song of the Holy Ones contains the spark of this same fire of creation. This is clearly the God of Milton:

> "Eä! Let these things Be! And I will send forth into the Void the Flame Imperishable, and it shall be at the heart of the World, and the World shall be; and those of you that will may go down into it." and suddenly the Ainur saw afar off a light, as it were a cloud with a living heart of

---

past and the Big Bang theory is in any way causal, but the implication of unity in such expressions as "The One," with the relationship to the nature of the Self may be archetypal.

[1] Franz, *C. G. Jung: His Myth in Our Time*, pp. 142–43.

[2] Milton, *Paradise Lost*, Book VII, ll. 243–49, 254–57.

flame; and they knew that this was no vision only, but that Ilúvatar had made a new thing: Eä, the World that Is.[3]

With this blinding imagery, a new world is subcreated. *The Silmarillion* provides a history for the peoples of Middle-earth that stretches back to the creation and beyond. The Elder Days are rich in symbol. The Children of God are young, the earth green, and the guardian agents of God (Ilúvatar or Eru) walk the land. These are the *Valar*, demiurgic creations of the thought of The One, who have unknowingly created the world out of their holy song and glimpsed at least a part of its future course. To them is entrusted the stewardship of creation and the welfare of the Children of God — Elves the Firstborn and Man the Lastborn. Their task is not easy, for mingled with their harmonious song is the seed of discord, personified by Melkor, first among the Valar.

His pride is strong, and he cannot accept domination; like Milton's Satan, he goes his own way, endlessly spoiling the efforts of the Guardians. Cast from his place among the Valar, his power is the seed of corruption, and he covets the realm prepared for the labors of the rest of the angelic host. Yet he was mightiest of the Holy Ones, and his independent strain was part of the thought of God. Grim his visage might be, but he is indisputably a creation of The One.

This is the philosophical problem of evil, a paradox which has bedeviled theologians for ages. The stubborn and preordained conclusion is to be found in the duality of God's nature. As God is an image projected by the psyche, so the form of God mirrors the form of the soul to which He is logically bound. The psyche is dual in nature, conscious and unconscious, dominated respectively by ego and shadow,

[3] Tolkien, *The Silmarillion*, p. 21.

symbolically light and dark, good and evil combined. Taoism distills this process into the yin and yang principles, the early proto-Christian Gnostics into the figure of a god frankly dual in personality, combining the opposing forces which pervade Man's phenomenal world. Tolkien is content with the brooding figure of Melkor, the fallen Ainu: he taints with the curse of entropy all that he touches, the nemesis of the creative synthesis of the Valar.

In his role as the shadow of God, Melkor struts and frets his overlong hour upon the stage, and his great feat is the destruction of the light of the Two Trees, Telperion and Laurelin, which gave light to the Land of the Valar. These glowing treasures were raised upon the mound of Ezellohar by Yavanna, the green-clad nature goddess of the Guardians. The chief contribution of the Two Trees to our story concerns the magical distillation of their light by Fëanor, cleverest of the Elves in the West:

> As three great jewels they were in form. But not until the End, when Fëanor shall return who perished ere the Sun was made . . . shall it be known of what substance they were made. Like the crystal of diamonds it appeared, yet was more strong than adamant, so that no violence could mar or break it . . . Yet that crystal was to the Silmarils but as is the body to the Children of Ilúvatar: the house of its inner fire, that is within it and yet in all parts of it, and is its life. And the inner fire of the Silmarils Fëanor made of the blended light of the Trees of Valinor, which lives in them yet, though the trees have long withered and shine no more.[4]

The symbols of tree and crystal will recur time and again in this discussion. The former is a symbol in many cases of

[4] Ibid., p. 78.

psychic growth, and we will see many examples of its power-ful use. The crystal, however, will have special significance in the history of Middle-earth. M. L. von Franz states:

> In many dreams the nuclear center, the Self . . . appears as a crystal. The mathematically precise arrangement of a crystal evokes in us the intuitive feeling that even in so-called "dead" matter there is a spiritual ordering principle at work. Thus the crystal often symbolically stands for the union of extreme opposites — of matter and spirit.[5]

But the silmarils are coveted by Melkor, the ancient foe. The endless strife of *The Silmarillion* — and, for that matter, the War of the Ring — really begins with the theft of the precious crystals and the ages of hopeless conflict as the Elves live out their doom trying to recover them. The great Elf-lords who turned their backs on the Valar in their pride and returned to Middle-earth from Aman the Blest did so bewil-dered by the desire of the treasures of Fëanor and bound by an oath that led them ineluctably on the path of tragedy. The history of the Elder Days is one of repeated alliance and es-trangement, war and betrayal, endless sorrow and cyclic re-birth. Evil is a given in the world, tears the inheritance of the Eldar "for long years numberless as the wings of trees."[6]

Yet there are moments of triumph, and these more often than not come with the chance (or predestined) union of Eldar and Edain, Elf-maiden and human hero. Together Beren and Lúthien regained a silmaril from the iron crown of the Great Enemy. Eärendil and Elwing, Lastborn and First-born, secured the intervention of the Valar in the last war in

---

[5] Franz, "The Process of Individuation" in *Man and His Symbols*, ed. C. G. Jung, p. 209.
[6] See Galadriel's lament, in Tolkien and Swann, *The Road Goes Ever On*, pp. 66–67.

which Melkor was finally cast out of the realm — and in their sons of mixed blood, Elros and Elrond, seemingly lies the future of the realm.

The brothers must make a choice: the Half-elven must select either the immortality of Elves (and the inevitable world-weariness that accompanies it through the burdensome oath of Fëanor) or accept the gift of Ilúvatar, the mortality of men. One realm is largely spiritual, backward-looking; in the other is death, but the world of men is the way of material wealth, earthly power, and majesty, and the future of Middle-earth. Elrond chooses the way of immortality and endless burden until the end of days. Elros picks the path of men, and he and his people are granted an island in sight of the Blessed Realm of the Valar.

Jealousy should not arise, for the possession of immortality is not an unalloyed blessing. Ultimately the Elves, one by one, are fated to forsake Middle-earth, the land of their creation and exile, and return to the West. But no matter how green and sunlit a world may be, it is bound to get old after a few thousand years, and to live in Middle-earth for only one age is to know sorrow and despair. "I have seen three ages in the West of the World, and many defeats, and many fruitless victories,"[7] complains Elrond, whose long-suffering manner should convince anyone that living forever is not all it is cracked up to be.

But life proves little better for Elros and his progeny. Though granted far longer life than lesser men, the Númenóreans begin to chafe under the smallness of their realm and the brevity of life after only a few long generations. They embark on conquests, and secure a foothold once more on Middle-earth. The free peoples are hardly in a position to complain, having tasted the bitter dominion of

[7] Tolkien, *The Lord of the Rings*, I: 234.

Sauron, former deputy to the Great Enemy, who has found easy pickings with the dwindling of the Elves and the departure of the strongest tribes of Men.

This *Drang nach Osten* is not the only force stirring the Númenóreans, however; the old problem of mortality gnaws away at them, spoiling the sweetness of wealth and empire. Kings who once went willingly to their deaths after the prime of life now cling gracelessly to existence well into senility, and their heirs have no choice but to conspire or twiddle their thumbs into middle age. Suspicion and hostility creep into their relations with the Elves, the kindred are sundered. Man is becoming Man, his ties to the past and the guardianship of the Valar are weakening. The one-sidedness of his culture is evidenced by his preoccupation with material wealth and the shadow of death.

In contrast to the prevailing mood of disillusionment and cynicism, a small group of Númenóreans who prefer to maintain the link with the past forms around Elendil and his sons. When the neurotic king Ar-Pharazôn the Golden rejects the foundations of Númenor, outlaws the Elvish tongue, and sets out to conquer the Uttermost West and win the prize of immortality, Elendil's party of the faithful remains behind.

This proves to be a fortunate choice. The Valar are always reluctant to meddle with Men, whose fate has not been revealed to them, and who go their own stubborn way without interference. Influencing the affairs of Men is like tampering with the ecology: no one knows what the final outcome will be. Consequently they wash their hands of guardianship for the duration of the war and leave the resolution of the conflict to The One. Ilúvatar destroys the Númenórean fleet and drowns their island kingdom, from the ruin of which only the scattered faithful escape.

But, as we are told in the *Akallabêth*, Númenor is reestablished in Middle-earth by Elendil and his sons, Isildur and

Anárion: a southern kingdom, Gondor, and a northern realm, Arnor. The kingdom is not bought without pain: Sauron has arisen once again to challenge the Children of God. The Last Alliance brings together the armies of the Númenóreans and the Elves of Middle-earth; Sauron is defeated, his citadel cast down, his armies annihilated, his ring of power cut from his finger and claimed as weregild by Isildur for the death of his father. Isildur is finally ambushed and slain and the treacherous ring slips from his finger into the Great River.

An uneasy peace, the *Pax Gondorensis*, reigns in Middle-earth through much of the Third Age, though the North Kingdom is finally lost and the fortunes of the Númenóreans suffer both triumph and reverse. But seen in its entirety, the Third Age is a period of decline. The old order, the age-old alliance of Men and Elves, is fading. The former are too suspicious and preoccupied with wealth and power, the latter just too worn out with age after age of "many defeats and fruitless victories" to muster much excitement about the fate of Man. Many of the best and brightest of the Elves have made their journey to the judgment halls and endless repose of the West: Fëanor, who wrought the silmarils; Thingol, King of Doriath in the Elder Days; Lúthien, nightingale of her people; Gil-Galad, last High King of the Elves of Middle-earth. Alliance with men is a fleeting venture, and the results always seem to benefit the mortals far more than the People of the Stars. The Dwarves, of course, are quite impossible, worse even than Men: grouchy, stubby, stingy and vindictive, they are at best fit companions for Men; and the two are welcome to share Middle-earth to their hearts' content!*

---

* An attitude that still puzzles me, and a sign that the Elves' chief weakness, other than their undercurrent of *Weltschmerz*, is that they take themselves too seriously. *The Silmarillion* suggests that the Dwarves hardly de-

This is the historical setting for *The Lord of The Rings*. The kingdom of Men has fallen on shabby times. As before, the heritage of the past, Man's link to the creators, has faded. The symptoms are clear: the preoccupation with conquest and riches that finished Númenor, the enervative materialism, the endless intramural wars and conspiracies that ultimately devastate Arnor, the corruptive power and gradual weakening of Gondor. The symbol of the past and present is the King, and his sign is the White Tree saved from the wreck of Númenor.

The White Tree is an important symbol of growth and transcendence. It has its roots in the ground and its branches spread toward the heavens. The Norse people of a millennium ago visualized the heavens and the underworld as joined by Yggdrasíl, the world tree; at its base (ground level) lay Midgard, Middle-earth, the realm of Men. In the case of Tolkien's world, the White Tree affirms, by its descent from the luminous trees of the Valar in the Uttermost West, the origin of Men and the role of The One. It binds conscious and collective unconsciousness in Middle-earth. As long as the White Tree lives, Man's psyche is balanced and whole.

The withering of the tree is symptomatic of the centuries of decay and grief in Gondor, culminating in the death of the last king of the line of Anárion. In the veins of the King is the blood of the Lords of Númenor, the blood of Eärendil and Elwing, in which the opposites are united. With the failure of that line, withered tree and vacant throne, Gondor's decline proceeds from outside and from within.

The arrangement of the world after the fall of Morgoth at the end of the First Age was perfectly balanced, and in the loss of this balance is the root of Gondor's problems. The

---

serve all the blame for the feud, and saved the Elves' cause on more than one occasion.

pattern may be visualized in the disturbed symbolic form of the yin-yang. Elrond chose the fate of the Eldar, and dwells in Middle-earth; Elros assumed the gift of Men and established his kingdom within sight of the Undying Lands. With the loss of Númenor the psyche of the West is suddenly unbalanced, the fleeting Selfhood of that golden age lost beneath the waves (in the depths of the unconscious). The renewal of the pact between conscious and unconscious symbolized by the King (as *coincidentia oppositorum*) and the promise of growth (the White Tree) have been carelessly frittered away as the price of one-sidedness.

Gondor under the ruling stewards continues its decline and pursuit of mundane power until the resurgence of Sauron. This is, in the analogy of the individual psyche, the first hint of impending trouble — Middle-earth's ever-present shadow takes visible shape again, and Man's journey through the fog of history is once more troubled by the frightful fiend.

In *The Spiritual Problem of Modern Man* and other commentaries, Jung discussed this matter of cultural one-sidedness at some length. He deplored the dwindling of conscious symbols for expression of unconscious promptings and despised the chaotic or fragmented nature of modern art when cut loose from the archetypal patterns of wholeness. The problem of one-sidedness is distilled in this idea: simple denial of the unconscious aspects of the psyche does not make them go away — it may indeed cause them to grow more powerful than ever, bringing us increasingly, if unwillingly, under their sway.

Sauron the Dark Lord (darkness is frequently a symbol of the unconscious), the shadow of Middle-earth, waxes as Man's spirit wanes. The preoccupation of Gondor with material matters, the denial of the emblems that gave Gondor strength serve only to strengthen the shadow. Ignoring the

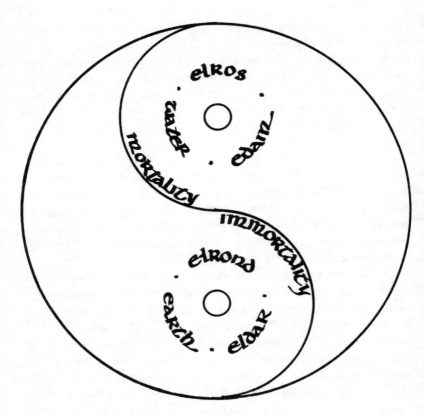

FIGURE 8. ELROS AND ELROND

evolution of Man and its unconscious vestiges causes their personification in the Dark Lord to become more powerful than ever.[8]

This is the sort of psychic fragmentation — what Jung calls the "sickness of dissociation"[9] — that heralds the emergence of the long repressed and denied unconscious complexes, powerfully numinous (from *numen*) remnants of the past. Arnor and its fall reflect this decay of the psyche. The northern kingdom, ruled by the descendants of Isildur, soon fell apart into petty kingdoms: Arthedain, Cardolan, Rhudaur. Some maintained their roots in the Elder Days; others fell slowly under the power of unconscious complexes, symbolized in this dream world by the Witch-King of Angmar. The loss of spirit is traced in the gradual decline in glory and power of the North, which ends with a whimper at the passing of the last king. The mansions, palaces, and markets of Fornost become ruins and grassy mounds; thorns grow in its courtyards, owls and foxes make their abode in its shattered towers. The line of Isildur, the noble strain of Elros Star-Foam, is resigned to a fugitive, nomadic existence. That it lives on at all is through its reluctance to yield to despair. It clings to the heirlooms of a proud past, fends off despair with a broken sword, and nurtures its hope. It reveres the past, survives the present, and awaits the future.

Hobbits are the essence of human strength and human frailty, even more than the Men of Tolkien's world. The Shire is Middle-earth in microcosm, and the central features of the world's ills are to be found in Hobbiton, under hill and by water.

The Shire of the Third Age was not a bad place to live:

---

[8] "Everyone carries a shadow, and the less it is embodied in the individual's conscious life, the blacker and denser it is." Jung, *Psychology and Religion: West and East*, p. 76.
[9] Jung, *Civilization in Transition*, p. 141.

protected, serene, and well-nourished. It was certainly suited to the likes and dislikes of hobbits:

> And there in that pleasant corner of the world they plied their well-ordered business of living, and they heeded less and less the world outside where dark things moved, until they came to think that peace and plenty were the rule in Middle-earth and the right of all sensible folk. They forgot or ignored what little they had ever known of the Guardians,* and of the labours of those that made possible the long peace of the Shire.[10]

Decent, respectable hobbits were, in fact, as dull as possible. They certainly did not long for adventure, having enough to keep themselves entertained with the mundane chores of agriculture and free enterprise, and enough fun to be had draining a mug of beer at *The Green Dragon* or the *Ivy Bush* after a hard day's labor. Their concern with conscious matters was so complete that hints of anything out of the ordinary — "the world outside where dark things moved" — was brushed aside impatiently whenever it intruded. Their roots were deep in the land but shallow in the psyche, and they were without conscious outlet for deeper motives. Their religion — "what little they had ever known of the Guardians" — had been discarded, and the suggestion of the Dark Lord and the Land of Mordor, threatening symbols of the shadow and its realm, was "a shadow on the borders of old stories."[11] An early scene in *The Fellowship of the Ring*, which

---

* A reference to the Valar which is not elaborated upon, nor linked to any other character or situation. There is no organized description of religion in *The Lord of the Rings* other than the hymns of the Elves and the moment of silence observed by Faramir and the Rangers of Ithilien in *The Lord of the Rings*, II: 251. This reference to its abandonment is ample evidence of its once and future importance.

[10] Tolkien, *The Lord of the Rings*, I: 16.

[11] Ibid., I: 57.

could be dismissed as mere donnish whimsy, may be far more significant in the setting of the stage for the ordeals that follow than the casual reader might imagine. The redoubtable Sam Gamgee holds forth in a Bywater inn on a spring evening on the subject of the world outside: "Queer things you do hear these days, to be sure."

> "Ah," said Ted [Sandyman, the miller's son], "you do, if you listen. But I can hear fireside-tales and children's stories at home, if I want to."
>
> "No doubt you can," retorted Sam, "and I daresay there's more truth in some of them than you reckon. Who invented the stories anyway? Take dragons now."
>
> "No thank 'ee," said Ted, "I won't. I heard tell of them when I was a youngster, but there's no call to believe in them now. There's only one Dragon in Bywater, and that's Green," he said, getting a general laugh.[12]

Jung regarded fairy stories as sources rich in unconscious materials (excluding by definition those "children's stories" that are really written for adults) that need not be bound by the symbolically impoverished intellectual domains of one-sided adulthood. Ted Sandyman brushes aside the unacceptable encroachments of the world outside his calm and conscious fool's paradise. Sam, uneducated but introspective, has some inkling of the hidden truth in these tales, more than Ted and his workaday chums reckon.

Sam's choice of dragons is interesting. The dragon is a fantastic beast which carries very powerful and specific aspects of transcendence in its form. It figures, as we shall see, in Bilbo's personal growth. But Ted won't have any of Sam's dragons, things he had heard tell of when he was a youngster but has subsequently outgrown. Mistaking form for content,

[12] Ibid., I: 51.

he relegates the potent dragon-image to the trash heap: "there's no call to believe in them now." In the one-sided existence of the Shire, there *is* no call — the call is muted, the provocative archetypal urgings, the faint horns of Elfland, have no sympathetic conscious chord. Like most of those who have had the fortune to live in times of spiritual deprivation, to recognize the loss is to be an outsider.

Sam, the rustic but sensitive pupil of Bilbo Baggins, has learned his symbols along with his letters. He senses the impending change from which his insulated pals in the pub are still defended by layers of repression. Sam's feet, though he scarcely recognizes it, have already turned onto the road, the great road of which all others are but tributaries — the road to the Grey Havens.

IV

the individuated hobbit

BILBO BAGGINS of Bag End was as conventional a hobbit as any other — despite the influence of his scandalous mother — and, like his conservative associates, eschewed adventure in all its distasteful forms. The most dangerous adventure of all, of course, is the journey into one's own psyche; and it is just that adventure that Bilbo undertakes in the fiftieth year of his life.

Nor is he really dragged kicking and screaming by the wizard and thirteen Dwarves. As they sang of the silence and majesty, the gleaming crystal columns and torchlit halls of the Lonely Mountain, Bilbo felt a stirring in his heart:

> Then something Tookish woke up inside him, and he wished to go and see the great mountains, and hear the pine-trees and the waterfalls, and explore the caves, and wear a sword instead of a walking stick.[1]

But this glimpse of the shadow world, the sudden revealing of a forgotten strain of Tookishness, is too much for this watchful, timid hobbit consciousness:

[1] Tolkien, *The Hobbit*, pp. 25–26.

> Suddenly in the wood beyond The Water a flame leapt
> up — probably somebody lighting a wood fire — and he
> thought of plundering dragons settling on his quiet Hill
> and kindling it all to flames. He shuddered; and very
> quickly he was plain Mr. Baggins of Bag End, Under-Hill,
> again.[2]

The potency of these newly awakened symbols is so compelling that Bilbo must suppress the strange and disquieting
feelings they evoke, unbidden, from the depths of what
serves a hobbit for an unconscious. The Tookishness sub-
sides.

This "Tookishness" is explicitly personified as the "fabu-
lous Belladonna Took," Bilbo's mother. It is a female figure;
a magical, potent figure out of Faërie, and the author and
manipulator of his urges to climb above his humdrum hobbit
existence. It is also his link with the collective past — the
narrator speculates that some hobbit in the Took genealogy
must have taken a fairy (Elvish) wife, another reference to
the mystical and reverential, dimensions quite foreign to
hobbit affairs. This is the first inkling that Bilbo is about to
break out of his one-sided life, and it frightens him. Well it
might, for even in the brave departure from the Shire, "run-
ning as fast as his furry feet could carry him,"[3] he could not
have guessed what horrors lay ahead. How many hobbits of
his generation had been obliged to deal with trolls, or seen
trolls, or even believed in them? Only Bilbo, one presumes.

And fearsome trolls they are. Bilbo's world is a dream
world, a Faerie world; and in the world of dreams, of the
psyche, the aggressive animal may symbolize unrestrained
libido.[4] The trolls, although nominally anthropomorphic,

---

[2] Tolkien, *The Hobbit*, p. 26.
[3] Ibid., p. 38.
[4] Jung, *Symbols of Transformation*, p. 328.

seem to fall into this functional category — if there was ever inarticulate, unrestrained libido in action, it is the trio of Bert, Bill, and Tom. This may be regarded as the first sign of the power, the numinous potency, of the complexes that reside in Bilbo's unconscious.

Gandalf serves here as rescuer, but he is much more than that; I have reserved a separate chapter for this amazing personage. For now, he is the guide, good for an occasional flash of temper and magic. Later on he will serve a more dramatic purpose — his powers will mature.

The travelers' brief respite in Rivendell allows the interpretation of Thorin's map, and the secrets hidden in it by magic are revealed by Elrond. Elrond is a symbol of the union of opposites (Elf and Man); it is only logical that he should be the one to find the key to the map — the moon-letters, runes that are revealed only by moonlight. He brings forth the hidden instructions ("stand by the grey stone when the thrush knocks") from the depths of the unconscious, the clue which will unlock the secrets of the hidden psyche. The moon is often connected, at least in the male psyche, with the unconscious, as the sun may symbolize in men's dreams and imagination the conscious.

After their departure from Rivendell, wizard, Dwarves, and hobbit are confronted by a mountain storm; the sudden fury and flashes of lightning portend symbolically the approach of a sudden psychic change, and the change which is about to occur is the most dramatic and significant of all.

Bilbo's progress thus far has only hinted at the coming crisis, the first stirrings of a change that may express the symptoms of neurosis; but this is not the real psyche, only a dream psyche. The appearance of certain portents, numinous images charged with inflated power that surge from the depths of the unconscious, serve as warnings — warnings that invariably make Bilbo long for the solid comfort of his hobbit-hole. The last thing Mr. Baggins wants to undertake at this point is a journey Under Hill into the depths of his forgotten mind and a confrontation with the unlovely demons of the imagination that lurk there. Attention is reversed now, from an outward to an inward perspective, and the frightful fiend is thus ahead rather than behind. But with thirteen Dwarves pulling him on and a wizard standing rear guard to head off any thoughts of malingering, Bilbo must march on.

Descent may symbolize the direction of attention and energy into the unconscious, and this is where Bilbo is dumped unceremoniously during the party's headlong flight from the pursuing mountain goblins. Lost and alone, he stumbles exhausted, and his hand finds — by chance? — the Ring.

Imagine yourself groping blindly about the darkness of your own unconscious, uncertain of what direction to take. Directing your efforts is *you*, as you know yourself — the ego complex. But the ego is conscious, and is treading unfamiliar paths. You are only dimly aware now, after signals granted you in dream and vision, of the presence of another *you* — forgotten, ignored, reflexively denied, buried far from the light of day. It is both you and not-you, noman and everyman, your constant companion on the foggy road.

"Deep down here by the dark water lived old Gollum, a small slimy creature."[5] Tolkien professes ignorance of Gollum's origins in *The Hobbit*. But we shall learn later that old Gollum is, or was, Sméagol, a hobbit who dwelt ages ago by the banks of the Great River. The very idea is repulsive to Frodo when he first hears of it, years later: "How loathsome! . . . I can't believe that Gollum was connected with hobbits, however distantly . . . what an abominable notion!"[6] Here-

---

[5] Tolkien, *The Hobbit*, p. 77.
[6] Tolkien, *The Lord of the Rings*, I: 60.

tofore Gollum was only a slimy, unlovely curiosity; now he is much more threatening, the image of the nightmare not-hobbit, the alter ego that lurks just out of sight.

Gollum paddles about his little cold pool of water deep at the mountain's roots. The deep water is associated symbolically with the unconscious, with depth and knowledge and wisdom. Bilbo's progress has thus been *descent* into the *unconscious*, in the first timid search for enlightenment. But true wisdom for Bilbo must be shunted aside — the first order of business is to get out of that mountain as soon as possible. The revelations of the unconscious are really too much! The key to escape is slimy old Gollum, repulsive though he may be. Their riddle game is a duel of conscious and unconscious preoccupations. Bilbo marshals images of an egg (symbolizing the eye of the conscious), eating (material world), sun on the daisies (*sol* as representation of the conscious); Gollum relies upon contrasting pictures: wind, darkness, the roots of mountains, fish. But Bilbo is careless and fated to be anything but rid of Gollum, whatever the outcome of the riddle game. He gives Gollum his *name* — an important piece of information not to be blurted heedlessly to anyone, much less a mildewy green-eyed figure of shadow who lives in a cave, eats raw goblins caught unawares, and talks to himself. And Bilbo, above all, has the Ring, in whose shining symmetry is encased Gollum's dark soul.

No, Bilbo is never free of Gollum, and never quite breaks away from that riddle game under the mountain. Symbolically this is the pivot point of the story, and the most powerful juxtaposition of forces. It clearly moved the author, since Tolkien was never quite content to leave this haunting episode behind until it had been elaborated and resolved many years and three volumes later. In the Jungian sense, this is a confrontation of immense potential, so much that it has enthralled countless readers, fascinated by its stark primordial imagery and the sympathetic chord in the readers' collective soul.

Bilbo is clearly the ego, as the focal personality thus far in the story. More than this, Bilbo is the reader's ego. Bilbo's adventure has become the reader's dream, his creative, vicarious inner experience. The ego has courageously (more or less) entered the forbidden recesses of the unconscious and collided unexpectedly with its dark mirror image. The collision is brief and incomplete — the two are now for the first time fully aware of each other's existence, and their fates are inseparably bound. The only possible end of this dream lies many years and many miles ahead, at the Cracks of Doom.

Ego and shadow face each other at the twilit border of dark and light, and they are tied together by a precious ring, the One Ring, the "One Ring to find them/One Ring to bring them all and in the darkness bind them." This is the ruling Ring, for it rules both their fates; and these fates are bound, as is foretold, "in the Land of Mordor where the Shadows lie."[7]

We have already noted in the previous chapter on Jungian theory that individuation and Self-realization are not achieved by the conquest and destruction of the shadow. Only more one-sidedness is at the close of that battle, for the shadow is a necessary part of the psyche, the source of creativity as well as darker impulse. Old Gollum, in any case, for all his gulping evil unwholesome ruminations, cowardice, and endless autistic self-pity, is not all bad. Years later, Gandalf parries Frodo's instinctive revulsion and vindictiveness:

> He had proved tougher than even one of the Wise could have guessed — as a hobbit might. There was a little

---

[7] Tolkien, *The Lord of the Rings*, I: 57.

corner of his mind that was still his own, and light came through it, as through a chink in the dark: a light out of the past.*[8]

But Frodo needs a lot of convincing. Gollum is still part of the picture, and he can never be brushed aside without endangering the preordained balance of the psyche. It is clear at least to the perceptive that Gollum has a role to play in the coming drama. I personally find Gollum one of the most sympathetic figures in the story. He is indeed a key actor in the play, and it may not be fair to cast him in a role of shadow. It might be just as accurate to call him an ego dominated by dark impulse but finally capable of being driven in desperation to some slender virtue or hair-raising vice as the scenario dictates, just as Bilbo and Frodo are ego personifications easily inclined to the light but ever aware of the dark shadow vestige which may emerge at critical moments. Bilbo is capable of spinning tall tales about his "precious" just as Gollum does, without thinking. And Frodo, everyone's hero, really fails the test at the dramatic moment, and must be rescued by his slithering, unwilling shadow.

I am, of course, dancing lightly about the truly central (literally and figuratively) issue of the Ring. The Ring is the focal point of the *symbolic* story, and as such subtly overwhelms the overt plot like the latent content of a dream that belies the manifest experience. To say that either *The Hobbit* or *The Lord of the Rings* is a tale of there and back again is to suggest that the *Divine Comedy* is a book about cave exploring. Tolkien's faërie world is a world of light and dark, a realm with very few softer tones (and whenever a character

---

[8] Ibid., I: 61.
* We might suppose that Gollum possessed a dark, antisocial ego and a compensating prosocial shadow.

seems to assume a mantle of grey ambivalence, the cause is invariably the Ring). At the border is the twilight, the furthest marches of the conscious, where things are not as they seem; and binding these realms together is the precious Ring.

The Ring is perfect in form, and stands for the Self — the Ruling Ring, that is to say, is the way in which the archetype of the Self-in-potentia personifies itself. Critics have compared the Ring to Andvari's treasure in *der Ring des Nibelungen*.[9] This is an interesting comparison, but falls short of the essential symbolic contribution of the precious.

The Ring's symmetry is perfectly balanced, a graceful circle, distilling the concepts of balance and perfection and the union of all opposites that will characterize the Self after its realization. Its material is gold, because of its incorruptible nature as in the philosophy of alchemy. Jung was fascinated by the complex and powerful imagery of medieval alchemy and the theology of the proto-Christian Gnostics, and we will examine the appearance of a variety of symbolic conventions from these sources. He believed that the alchemic and Gnostic symbolic sources, with their recognition of the importance of balance, opposition, and compensation, were psychologically more satisfying than the meager imagery of Protestantism in particular or western Christianity in general.[10] In any case, the form and function of the Ring are not left in doubt. The Ring's fate is etched inside and out in fiery letters:

One Ring to rule them all, One Ring to find them.
One Ring to bring them all and in the darkness bind them.[11]

---

[9] Noel, *Mythology of Middle-earth*, pp. 157–59.
[10] Jung, *Symbols of Transformation*, p. 441.
[11] Tolkien, *The Lord of the Rings*, I: 57.

The Ring is the Self, the potential force that promises finally to make whole both hobbit and Middle-earth.

But Bilbo is not through spelunking — ahead lie the Lonely Mountain and a far more formidable foe than wretched Gollum. Bilbo must now earn his title of burglar — or "expert treasure-hunter," as he would doubtless prefer to be called — by dickering with Smaug the Mighty, "greatest and chiefest of catastrophes."

The dragon is a common symbol in the mythologies of a variety of times and cultures. In form, it is a fusion of serpent, bird, and other animals, and I cannot resist digressing for a few paragraphs in honor of this fantastic beast and its importance in understanding the imagery of the psyche.

The winged snake is encountered in odd places. The medical profession in this country has embraced the caduceus as its symbol. This is actually an error — the proper symbol, and that which is used elsewhere, is the staff of Asklepios, a stick about which is entwined the single serpent. I shall not bother with the mythological basis for this emblem, since it does not influence our present concerns; but the caduceus, whether it is appropriate for the medical profession or not, gives us a hint about winged snakes in general.

The caduceus is the winged staff of Hermes, the Greek god who served as messenger and patron of travelers. He is also the intermediary between gods and the underworld; unifier of light and darkness, his common symbol being the phallic *herm* placed at crossroads. He is also the guide of dead souls, which is not encouraging for patients whose doctors embrace his staff. The symbolic nature of the caduceus is fairly straightforward: the serpents are chthonic, earthy, close to the underworld, suggestive of Man's lowly phylogenetic origins. The wings reflect the soaring soul of Man, the consciousness that sets him apart from his scaly and furry forefathers. The central staff binds the two together — mating snakes, the instinctual substrate, flying bird, the sunlit potential of consciousness.

The union of opposites is thus an essential part of such figures, among which we must place the dragon. Those familiar with mythology will point out that the Serpent of Midgard, who gnawed for ages at the roots of the Norse world tree Yggdrasil, was a "worm": creeping and wingless. Remember, however, that he was compensated (as was the rest of the complex Norse world) by the eagle that perched in the top branches of the tree. The two symbols are not yet fused, and carry on no more than a spirited dialogue through the good offices of a squirrel whose fate it is to scamper up and down Yggdrasil's loftiness from one to the other until the day of Ragnarökk.

But Smaug the Mighty is a full-fledged (should one say "fledged"? His wings are batlike and featherless) fire-drake, long of tooth, broad of wing, bad of breath, and shudderingly articulate.

Tolkien, for some reason which will remain unguessed, was very nonevaluative in his general treatment of dragons. The worms of *The Silmarillion* are a pretty grim lot, true; but then there is little frivolity about that work, composed of the tear-soaked chronicles of the Eldar's trials in Middle-earth. I have already made clear to the reader that I am not impressed by the Elves' studious garment-rending and hand-wringing. Had they bothered to stop and talk for a few moments with any of the dragons set against them, they might have found entertainment enough to offset the confounded eternal weariness of the world. When Tolkien removes his Elvish persona and confronts dragons as the plucky hobbit or the sturdy yeoman-farmer, worms fare better. *Chrysophylax Dives* is merely living up to his miserly name, and doing so with wit, gusto, and a pinch of pathos. Smaug is certainly not to be trifled with, and admittedly dealt rather summarily with the Dwarves in the time of Thrain; but he is older now and perceptibly more mellow, at least willing to chat for a while before belching napalm and ending meaningful dialogue. And if he is greedy, well, that is what dragons are supposed to be; we cannot blame him for that, nor expect altruism of a fire-drake any more than empathy from a weeping crocodile. I really find Smaug altogether more worthy of sympathy than some hobbits — Lobelia Sackville-Baggins would have smitten the pesky lizard with a furled umbrella and sent him off whimpering. But perhaps after all pestiferous and acquisitive relatives are more likely to interrupt our serenity in contemporary times than thundering dragons.

Bilbo is terrified. Sting and Ring are hardly more than lucky charms in the great treasure cave, not proof against the fearful flamethrower. Smaug is what we of Othello's trade call an area weapon: precise location of the target is not required, nor is fastidious marksmanship necessary for good terminal effect. But Bilbo has guts that belie his species' reputation. None of the Dwarves, not even the venerable, much-decorated Thorin Oakenshield, who proved his mettle in the Goblin Wars, has volunteered to help him burgle treasure with the dragon so near. As he treads the tunnel coming ever nearer to the uninviting red glow the "least Tookish part of him" wavers, wishing yet again for the comfy hole at Bag End.

This is the persona (the "good decent hobbit") railing impotently at the anima (the Tookish part, personified as the great Belladonna, from whom he has surely inherited the propensity for disturbing sleeping dragons); but the objections are too little and much too late. He is committed to the path of Self-realization, like it or not. In fact, the controlled social mask is already slipping away, no longer supported by the need to maintain a reputation for the neighbors.

The nature of Bilbo's journey across the landscape of the psyche is revealed by his reply to Smaug's inquiry: "Who are you and where do you come from, if I may ask?"

> "You may indeed! I come from under the hill, and under the hills and over the hills my paths led. And through the air. I am he that walks unseen."

Over hill and under hill, indeed; Bilbo is too modest (if that is posible). "I am the friend of bears [a reference to Beorn, the theriomorphic figure we will discuss in more detail later] and the guest of eagles. I am Ringwinner and Luckwearer . . . [12]

This is a complex and pregnant sort of name. It traces his path through conscious and unconscious (over hill and under hill) that has led him this far; establishes his foundation in both worlds ("friend of bears" — i.e., chthonic, earthy, bound to the animal shadow, the instinctive foundation of the psyche; and "guest of eagles" — one who may also soar at will in the light of consciousness). He glories in his new position as pivotal figure in the drama, the link between worlds (Ringwinner) and the key to fortune (Luckwearer) by possession of the magical transcending treasure.

But Bilbo succumbs to a near fatal weakness at this critical point. He has in the euphoria of the moment reveled too thoughtlessly in Belladonna's triumph, ignored the conscious part of him, which would have been more cautious and circumspect in talking to dragons. Smaug is sure-footed in the dark world, he has dwelt there long; Bilbo is a stranger in the perilous realm, and he has barely stepped into it before the incautious foot is thrust in his mouth, tipping off the worm to dangerous details of the plan. *"Thief* in the *Shadows!"* *

---

[12] Tolkien, *The Hobbit*, pp. 212–13.
* Italics mine.

snarls the beast, "my armour is like tenfold shields, my teeth are swords, my claws spears, the shock of my tail a thunderbolt, my wings a hurricane, and my breath death!"[13]

This uncouth outburst is one that reveals the volume and fury of the long-repressed libido, the surging, powerful energy that has for so long been denied conscious symbolization. Smaug has for the moment ceased to be a transcendental, transforming symbol and become pure animal power, untamed psychic drive. But transforming symbol is his major role still, the winged serpent, and like St. George, Bilbo must slay or outwit the beast to pave the way for the Self's advent. He has already done this, though he has no way of knowing it, with his careless clues — Smaug is soon up and around for the first time in years, and Bilbo has provided the clue through the help of the magic thrush that allows Bard the Bowman to finish the monster and quench his flames. The black arrow pierces the gap in Smaug's armor, and the treasure is now lying unguarded in the darkness under the mountain.

Now, as Bilbo and the Dwarves begin their greedy inventory of the reclaimed wealth, there is a significant discovery. Bilbo, unknown to Thorin and company, has found the Arkenstone, Heart of the Mountain. "Indeed there could not be two such gems, even in so marvellous a hoard, even in all the world."[14] It is a perfect crystalline gem, a sparkling pale globe of light, the most cherished heirloom of the Dwarves of Erebor.

It is related in symbolism to the *lapis philosphorum*, the Philosopher's Stone of alchemy, which contains within its perfect symmetry the means of unifying the opposites, and means of transforming base metals into gold (also a union of opposites). In Jungian terms, it is a symbolic realization of

---

[13] Ibid., p. 215.
[14] Ibid., p. 224.

the Self through individuation:

> The goal of individuation, as pictured in unconscious images, represents a kind of mid-point or center in which the supreme value and the greatest life-intensity are concentrated. It cannot be distinguished from images of the supreme values of the various religions. It appears as naturally in the individuation process as it does in the religions . . . a four-square city or garden . . . as the *imago Dei* in the soul, as the "circle whose periphery is nowhere and whose center is everywhere," as a crystal, a stone, a tree, a vessel or a cosmic order . . .[15]

Certainly its location, deep in the treasure cave at the mountain's roots, suggests its abode in the unconscious. Now it is more than a potential: it, like the Ring, is in Bilbo's "pocketses."

It does not remain there long, of course, and Bilbo uses this barter to resolve the political impasse between the Elves and Lakemen on one side and the Dwarves, "under bewilderment of the treasure," on the other. The Arkenstone is both symbol and instrument of his new-found Self; he blends now the pragmatic hobbit of the Shire with the courage and vision of the Tookish adventurer.

Indeed, the little burglar has retrieved more from the dragon's hoard than golden chalices and glittering jewels; his treasure is the treasure of the Self, beside which the wealth of the King under the Mountain, the splendor and worldly pomp and lucre are small change. At the last he has no use for more of this gold than his small measure — enough to be a well-to-do hobbit and live out his life in comfort and contemplation at Bag End (or so he believes). Bilbo Baggins will never be the same. The prosaic gentlehobbit is now poetic as

---

[15] Franz, *C. G. Jung: His Myth in Our Time*, pp. 73–74.

well, his stuffy constricting persona shed (and Old Belladonna silenced), and the realization of his full potential within reach.

"My dear Bilbo!" observes Gandalf. "Something is the matter with you! You are not the hobbit that you were."[16]

[16] Tolkien, *The Hobbit*, p. 281.

V

"frodos dreme"

THE PUBLICATION of *The Hobbit* in 1939 did not, as we know, end Professor Tolkien's romance with his furry-footed subcreations. But in the technical sense the vast work that was to follow is not accurately described as a "sequel" to the slender story of Bilbo's adventure. *The Lord of the Rings* does not differ significantly in point or plot from the earlier work, a fact which more than one reviewer has noted. The themes have been changed slightly to fit a story of greater maturity, and the characters shifted and sometimes renamed — and the grand quest is placed on a somewhat loftier plane than burglary — but the plot structure is there in full and the symbolic structure is nearly identical.

Yet this does not detract from the greater story, nor yet diminish the charm of *The Hobbit*. In the expansion of his first hobbit story, Tolkien has added not only bulk but power. His first excursions into the psyche were "only essays in the craft, before it was full-grown,"[1] like the lesser rings fashioned by the smiths of Eregion.

[1] Tolkien, *The Lord of the Rings*, I: 53.

The Ring is the link between the two stories; and, as the Ring gives power according to the stature of its bearer, the new story is granted greater power. In *The Hobbit*, both conscious and unconscious were rather diminutive and occasionally comical. Comparing the mood of the two is like comparing Disney to Perrault. Bilbo was usually more "flummoxed" than consumed by terror, the dragon was really not such a bad fellow as long as you could dodge quickly, and Gandalf was merely an old conjurer with much dignity who could not bear looking ridiculous. The tale was peopled with small figures, whose small aims and penny-ante stakes could easily be contained by the smaller story. The higher purposes, the greater outcomes, were mere hints beyond the boundaries of an innocent excursion.

But now as Bilbo departs the Shire for the last time, the drama that once engrossed a few footsore Dwarves, a grumpy wizard, and a flummoxed hobbit has spread — and what was gossip in Hobbiton and Bywater now "troubles the councils of the Wise." Now that the unguessed origin of the Ring is beginning to come to light, more and more powers are being drawn into the terrifying vortex in the twilit borderland. The Ring is the most valued heirloom of the House of Isildur, seized from Sauron's finger as repayment for the death of Elendil of Westernesse. The fate of the West is bound up in the fate of the Ring, and the candle of Númenor may yet flicker and fail, devoured by the darkness of barbarism, the shadow of the frightful fiend.

In *The Hobbit* the foes were a loquacious dragon and an obstreperous autistic troglodyte. Now the West is faced by an enemy with a capital "E." The confrontation has spread away from the Ring like ripples in a pool; but like those ripples it will finally rebound at the last to the Ring. Its influence is in the highest places: the high strivings of the White Council and the valiant stand of Gondor; in the plots and bitter ends of the Dark Lord. Still, at the center, the focus of this broader confrontation, will remain the pivotal microcatastrophe whose outcome will decide the fate of Middle-earth. There at the gate between light and dark, conscious and unconscious, are two disgruntled Halflings — Frodo and Gollum.

I have tried as this discussion progressed to keep some sort of graphic structure in the mind's eye of the reader, in the hope that the more confusing and abstract concepts might be kept in their logical relationships. Until now, we have dealt with fairly simple forms; but now we must deal with not only personifying but also transforming archetypes and their various conscious projections. At the highest level we have pictured Middle-earth as a map of the psyche, with both conscious and unconscious aspects. Faërie and its associations and inhabitants, with their dwindling link to Man's past, are placed figuratively in the unconscious, the present condition of Man in the conscious because of its one-sidedness. In the case of the West, this is really two kingdoms: Númenor, lost realm within sight of the Undying Lands (Faërie), and Gondor, the new Númenor in Middle-earth. The former is now a land vanished beneath the waves (in the collective unconscious, that is) of the Men of the West, symbolized by the gleaming towered citadel on the spur of the White Mountains. Transcending past and present, conscious and unconscious, are the

---

FIGURE 9. SEVEN STARS AND SEVEN STONES AND ONE WHITE TREE

The White Tree saved from the wreck of Númenor is a symbol of growth. The three crowns represent the remnant of the Faithful who re-established the Men of the West on Middle-earth: Elendil, and his sons Isildur and Anárion. The encircling lines are from the poem which chronicles the hierlooms of Westerness: "Tall ships and tall kings three times three/What brought they from the foundered land, over the flowing sea?/Seven stars and seven stones and one white tree."

King and the White Tree. The King is the union of opposites, heir of Elros Half-elven, in whose veins flowed the blood of both Faërie and Middle-earth. The White Tree's roots begin in the unconscious past, the heritage of Man, and the branches reach for the stars; the tree symbolizes life and growth, progression toward maturity and Self-realization.

Much of the power of this image resides in the special place of Man among the Children of God. The Elves, People of the Stars, as they were named by the Valar, are the First-born, but their power is waning. After long ages of strife and sorrow their time on Middle-earth is ending. Middle-earth was their birthplace, before the rising of sun or moon, when they walked in wonder beneath the light of stars. But their long years and wisdom are a curse, and the bright promise of the first days of the world empty and peopled with ghosts. Their heritage is endless war, respite, and defeat, and victories spoiled by loss. The fairest of their works, shining stones and rings of power, have in the end brought only wars and mourning for the lost, the forever tainted. The crowning glory of the Eldar when they dwelt within sight of the shining abodes of the Valar were the silmarils; and those distillations of the glory of Eldamar, handiwork of Fëanor, brought nothing save bitter exile. The Three Rings forged by the Elves of Eregion are nullified by the One Ring, which in their folly they helped Sauron to fashion.

Nor is there much help from the Lastborn. The once great cities of the Elf-friends are ruins and shapeless mounds, mournful desolation. The new breed of Man is estranged, suspicious, obsessed with its own ambitions and regrets. Though he is Lastborn, Man is the inheritor.

Middle-earth is his alone. His span of years is short, a fleeting afternoon to an Elf; but so hope is born anew with each generation, and the weariness of the Elves is spared Man. Death is indeed the gift of Ilúvatar, for what Man lacks in patience and wisdom he gains in tenacity and ambition.

The concerns of Faërie are buried year by year in the roots of the White Tree, but the future of Man lies in the stars beyond its topmost branches.

Without roots a tree will die. The White Tree is dead, its link with the nourishing soil of the past severed by the failing line of Anárion and its vital link to the Undying Lands. As the past is forgotten by all but the faithful, the power of the shadow grows.

The fate of the Eldar is connected with the moon, that of the Edain with the sun:

> Isil the Sheen the Vanyar of old named the Moon, flower of Telperion in Valinor; and Anar the Fire-golden, fruit of Laurelin, they named the Sun. But the Noldor named them also Rana, the Wayward, and Vása, the Heart of Fire, that awakens and consumes; for the Sun was set as a sign for the awakening of Men and the waning of the Elves, but the Moon cherishes their memory.[2]

Men were also called "the Night-fearers, the Children of the Sun."[3] The Sun is a frequent symbol of the conscious, the moon of the unconscious.

This theme is reflected in the names of the royal line of Númenor, which established itself on the shores of Middle-earth. The new kingdom on Middle-earth is founded by Elendil and his sons Isildur and Anárion. *Elendil* may have two meanings in the High Elvish: "Star-lover" and "Elf-friend." The former is probably the intended meaning, the latter a philologist's compulsive pun.* The followers of Elen-

---

[2] Tolkien, *The Silmarillion*, p. 117.

[3] Ibid., p. 122.

* An example of this manipulation is found in Celtic Irish tradition: the hero of the rebellious Firbolg serfs of Connacht was *Cinn Cait*, which could mean either "war-leader" or "cat-head", depending on one's dialect and political preference.

dil at the fall of Númenor called themselves Elendili, Elf-friends, since the context suggested this meaning. In either case, the star association is valid, since the root El (star) is common to both interpretations. The likelihood that this was preferred is underscored by the names of his sons. *Ithil* and *Isil* both derive from the word for moon, and *Anar* from sun. The star-lover is father to the sun and moon.

What is the rightful place, then, of Star-lover? The stars, in Elven lore, are crystalline vessels within which shines the Flame Imperishable — a notion we will discuss in greater detail later. As sun and moon stand in the psyche for conscious and unconscious, the crystal star is evocative of the primordial image of the Self, binder and transcender. The symbolic concept of the star as occupying the *center* position between sun and moon is made quite specific in one of Tolkien's earliest explorations of his mythology:

> *O! West of the Moon, East of the Sun*
> *Lies the Haven of the Star* . . .[4]

In the seed of Elendil the opposites are united.

The original name for Minas Tirith was Minas Anor, Tower of the Sun; for it stood in the West, where the sun set, and was the stronghold of Anárion. Balancing it in the East was Minas Ithil, Tower of the Moon,[5] which was raised by the heirs of Elendil on the far borders of Ithilien, on the very slopes of the Mountains of Shadow; it was occupied by Isildur.* This was an arrangement which made elegant psychic sense: the sun (conscious) counterbalancing the moon (unconscious). Both were controlled by Gondor, the twin cit-

---

[4] Carpenter, *J. R. R. Tolkien*, p. 84.
[5] Tolkien, *The Lord of the Rings*, III: 416.
* Ithilien means "Land of the Moon"; Anórien to the west is "Land of the Sun."

adels complementing and compensating one another in perfect equilibrium; and the link between the two was the fair city of Osgiliath, Citadel of the Stars and jewel of Elendil, which literally and figuratively bridged the two realms by spanning the River Anduin at their border.

But in the year 2000 the orcs of the Witch-King attacked out of the passes of Mordor and laid siege to Minas Ithil; two years later it fell, and its new name was Minas Morgul, Tower of Sorcery.[6] What has happened here is the emergence of a sudden negative aspect of the shadow. This conflict — a figurative neurosis — has been brewing up silently for years, as the magnificent Kings of Gondor turned more and more to material, worldly glory, and the darkness was increasingly ignored or denied. The moon side of Gondor is no longer a balancing, compensating function, but a threatening omen: a source of dread. Since the moon of the unconscious is now negative in aspect and subject to repression, the name of its balancing force, wielder of conscious defenses, must be changed. The fair Tower of the Sun becomes the Tower of Guard, Minas Tirith. Here is the first stirring of the War of the Ring; the first symptom of the collective neurosis that has been forming almost unnoticed in the one-sidedness of Gondor. This obsession with the conscious processes has allowed the inflation of the shadow into the frightful fiend. The activities of the ego are now defensive rather than compensating.

Where is the key to the door, now locked, between the conscious and unconscious, the key to the Self? Where is the power to heal? The answer is unexpected, and it comes as a dream within the dream of Middle-earth that troubles the sleep of the sons of the Ruling Steward of Gondor. To Fara-

[6] Ibid.

FIGURE 10. TOWER OF THE SUN, TOWER OF THE MOON

mir and Boromir, heirs of Denethor II, comes the vision of a voice out of the West:

> *Seek for the Sword that was broken:*
> *In Imladris it dwells;*
> *There shall be counsels taken*
> *Stronger than Morgul-spells.*
> *There shall be shown a token*
> *That Doom is near at hand,*
> *For Isildur's bane shall waken,*
> *And the Halfling forth shall stand.* [7]

At the risk of being pedantic, I think it might clarify matters to discard some of the dream imagery and state in plain language what the unconscious is trying to say:

"Seek the forgotten link with the past, the symbol of the reborn House of Elendil; for only then shall Gondor be made whole. It is to be found in the house of Elrond the Half-elven, brother of the founder of the line of Kings of Númenor. In what you will find there is the key to the danger that threatens you, the terror out of the Mountains of Shadow. There, too, you will see that the final resolution is near, for the token of Man reunited will be seen, and you would never believe me if I told you in whose hand it will lie!"

Or, in the language of the analytical psychologist:

"The cure for the anxiety you feel, the pain of your one-sidedness, is in Self-realization. Your ego-tactic of ignoring your unconscious underpinnings has served only to make them seem more alarming. Turn and face the darkness, the 'spectre of the Brocken'; help is at hand, for at the end of

---

[7] Tolkien, *The Lord of the Rings*, I: 236.

that battle the Self will emerge and the psyche will be reunited."

Isildur's bane has had an unlikely history since its dunking in the Great River. First it was plucked from the river's bottom by Déagol the Stoor; then his friend Sméagol throttled him and took the precious Ring for his own, and it drove him out of his home and to the brink of madness in the mountain's dark heart. Bilbo claimed it, used it for purposes according to his stature and wit; now it has fallen into the hands of Frodo, who has no idea of its perilous origins.

In the first chapters of *The Fellowship of the Ring* his complacence is shattered by Gandalf. The Ring is now a terrifying burden, and Frodo thinks wildly of giving it away, destroying it. Gandalf knows well, however, that despite the Ring's evil essence it is the key to the coming struggle and the hope of Self-realization of the West, with whose fate he is intimately concerned.

The task of prying Frodo loose from the beloved Shire is made easier by his growing sense of confinement. This feeling of approaching unease had infected Bilbo long before, when he felt "all thin, sort of *stretched*, if you know what I mean: like butter that has been scraped over too much bread. That can't be right. I need a change or something."[8] And Bilbo is correct. His problem is the same as the much larger problem of Middle-earth: he has stopped growing. Psychic development is in a constant state of change; Bilbo's has somehow stopped, he has stagnated in the dull and provincial Shire. He will never be the same hobbit that he was before his journey there and back again, but his progress toward the ultimate maturity is frustrated, he begins to feel once again the stirrings of impending change. This *malaise* is an important part of the development of neurosis. Bilbo and Frodo are

---

[8] Tolkien, *The Lord of the Rings*, I: 39.

close to the earth, unsophisticated, and — like most hobbits — uncomplicated by nature; yet they are stifled by the
Shire. Of this sort of personality, a theorist writes:

> Though myriads of individuals can exist without feeling
> out of sorts in this quagmire of collective opinions and col-
> lective routines, there are a number of people Jung called
> of a "higher" type, who for one reason or another in their
> lives have remained at a primitive level. These . . . have
> allowed a torpor to settle on their lives, and as a result of
> the narrowness of conscious outlook — a type of one-
> sidedness because they "could be" broader in outlook —
> they fall into neurosis.[9]

The key in this case is that the bridge to the unconscious has
been lost. Jung liked this metaphor for one-sidedness as well;
in discussing the plight of modern man, he stated that "today
these bridges are in a state of partial collapse."[10] The same
simile holds for Middle-earth in the larger sense: the original
mid-point of Gondor was Osgiliath, Citadel of the Stars; at
the time of the story the bridges have been thrown down.
With the bridge in disrepair, symbols are not available in the
conscious to link its dynamics to the collective unconscious
and its archetypes, and so relieve the potential of one-sidedness. What does the Shire have to offer one who has dickered
with dragons, traded riddles with a shadow, held in his hand
the sparkling Heart of the Mountain? "I want to see mountains again, Gandalf, *mountains* . . ." Gandalf senses the old
hobbit's distress and understands his dilemma.

Bilbo is parted with difficulty from the Ring — for it has
been with him for years, is part of his very psyche — but the

---

[9] Rychlak, *Introduction to Personality and Psychotherapy*, p. 171.
[10] Jung, *The Practice of Psychotherapy*, p. 123.

sight of the road and his companions fills him again with the spirit of growth, breaks the bond of the present, and urges both a pledge to the past (unconscious) and a promise of the future (psychic growth).

> *Now far ahead the Road has gone,*
> *And I must follow, if I can,*
> *Pursuing it with eager feet,*
> *Until it joins some larger way*
> *Where many paths and errands meet.*
> *And whither then? I cannot say.* [11]

Whither indeed?

Now Frodo feels the deep unease, kept just below the level of awareness: "He began to say to himself: 'Perhaps I shall *cross the River myself* one day.'* To which the other half of his mind always replied: 'not yet.' "[12] His preoccupation with strange things, with the white spaces of maps beyond the Shire's borders, with the movement of dark things, the visions of lofty mountains and pine forests, reflects his deep and scarcely understood dissatisfaction with the lack of available symbols for his unconscious urges. The earthy half of his personality has been denied, ignored for too long, and soon he must follow Bilbo in search of the Self.

I have called this chapter "Frodos Dreme" for two reasons. The reference is to a poem reproduced in *The Tolkien Reader* (attributed to the Red Book of Westmarch) bearing that marginal title, which we will discuss in its proper place. The content of the verses and their haunting tone remind us now,

---

[11] Tolkien, *The Lord of the Rings*, I: 43.
[12] Ibid., p. 50.
* Italics mine.

after so many specific references to situations, persons, and events that the story is not intended as an explicit description of the process of Self-realization. It is rather a fantasy, a sort of prose dream in which the unconscious is given room to parade its symbols at the author's whim. The fact that the symbolic structure is somewhat more meticulous than we would expect of more common mythic themes in literature and in the clinical environment does not weaken its impact on the reader. The unconscious is not educated in analytical psychology — quite the reverse — and we must make do with ready imagery and organization.

Thus warned, at least, not to search for archetypes under every stone, behind every tree, we may view the development of Frodos Dreme with something like scientific detachment. Bear in mind that the symbols are not random events, but are arranged in their proper order to provide a map of the psyche at least as accurate as Thorin's map of Wilderland.

Frodo's anxiety at the approach of his fiftieth birthday is suggestive of an important aspect of Jung's approach to the constructs of personality development. Freudians maintain that the nature of one's personality is firmly determined in most dimensions by adolescence, behavioral idiosyncrasies springing from the flow of libido during early childhood and the nature of ego formation and the resolution of the Oedipal situation. Jung's view is more optimistic for those who have somehow contrived to reach adulthood. The formation of one-sidedness is a natural result of growing up in our age and society. During youth (which lasts, in Jung's view, until about age thirty-five to forty) the consciousness is developed and expanded, very much at the expense of the unconscious. "Middle life" follows, and it is during this period that the unconscious begins to get restive, and individuation if it is to occur will begin. Frodo (allowing for the longer life-span of hobbits) has reached this point as had Bilbo before him. This is in rather striking contrast to Freudian and most neo-Freudian practice — Freud in particular based much of his theory on clinical experience with young adults.

So in terms of temporal patterning, Frodo is ripe for individuation. But in the larger sense his own individuation is the delicate bearing on which the greater Self-realization of Man turns; and this is what *The Lord of the Rings* is about. The joy of life in Middle-earth will become in the end Frodo's private tragedy, as the savior is often compelled to give up himself what he gives to others.

To understand the quality of the gift we must search in the past of Middle-earth, the early development of Man, and the most powerful of the archetypal figures, the Grey Pilgrim.

VI

WHITE LADY, DARK LORD, GREY PILGRIM

THE GUARDIANSHIP of Middle-earth and of the Children
of God was entrusted by The One to the Valar, holy offspring of his thought. These creator-gods were few in number, and not all enter into the course of history since the
Elder Days. Each was personified as male or female, the
supreme position resting with the King of Valinor and his
spouse, Manwë and Varda. Despite their power, they had at
the beginning of *The Lord of the Rings* intervened but seldom
in the fate of Middle-earth, and the form and fate of the
Children of God were not entirely in their hands. Both Elves
and Men were their concerns, for they were stewards of The
One; but following the revolt of the Noldor and the exile of
so many of the High Elves, the influence of the Valar was far
less direct.

Their wrath was awakened for the rescue of their wards in
the last great war of the Elder Days when Morgoth was at
last subdued, his great fortress of Thangorodrim reduced to
rubble, and his bitter spirit expelled from the realm. At the
approach of the armada of Ar-Pharazôn the Golden, they

washed their hands of the fate of Man and called upon Ilúvatar, who changed the face of the earth and drowned the island kingdom of the Númenóreans. Now, in the last days of the Third Age, the Guardians are all but forgotten among Men, save only in Gondor where at least the shell of the White Tree is still cherished.

The name of Elbereth (Varda) is still chanted by the High Elves, and still troubles the hearts of the servants of the Dark Lord. The old powers are still abroad, but muted; and the reason for this standoffishness of the Valar is the peculiar problem of Men.

As is told in *The Silmarillion*, the Valar are loath to meddle with Men. Men are strange creatures — unpredictable, impetuous, occasionally treacherous, and as easily tempted to vice as influenced by virtue. The alliances of Men and Elves have been fleeting things, fraught with sorrow for every measure of success. Always the plans of the Valar seem to go awry when Men are involved. Ilúvatar, who knows the fate of his chosen, has his own plans for this fatuous species; and in silent obedience, the Guardians refrain from direct involvement.

But the Men of Gondor, those who alone of Men have kept the faith, are overmatched. Sauron the Great is a foe beyond their power to resist alone. The Dark Lord was, ages ago, one of the Maiar, lesser Holy Ones.* These angelic entities were associated with the Valar, and shared a great measure of their power. Sauron was seduced to the side of Melkor, who was called Morgoth, the Dark Enemy. Sauron fought as his chief lieutenant, *castelain* of Thangorodrim. Unlike his master, Sauron escaped the wreck of Angband when

---

* The word may be associated with the Hindu *Maya*, the world illusion that is only the outward manifestation of the all-encompassing Brahma.

it was overthrown by the Valar — and proved to be the bane of Men and Elves for two long ages.

Middle-earth in the waning years of the Third Age is bound to the fate of Men, not Elves, whose power dwindles. This is the problem of the Valar: to oppose Sauron, when they are not sensitive to the world and ways of Men. The vigor that comes, as we have seen, from Man's mortality is the gift of The One, not His stewards. Man's phenomenal world is beyond them, an enigma. How can the Valar intervene without causing disaster?

Two years in a row I was treated to a Christmas sermon at West Point which dealt with this very paradox.

It seemed that there was once a colonel who lived at West Point, and who was alone in his quarters one evening during the Christmas holidays. It was a bitter cold evening, and the terrible piercing wind of December was howling up the Hudson Valley. He was startled out of his relaxed and introspective solitude by the dismaying sound of something soft striking the dining room window with some force. He quickly donned coat and hood and stepped out the side door to investigate.

The wind had driven a small flock of birds into the lee of the house; they were exhausted, buffeted by the pitiless wind and near the limits of endurance. The light beyond the window had attracted them, and one had tried to fly through the glass. The colonel was cold and miserable, but he concluded that the birds were far worse off than he, and would certainly not last the night without help. He opened the door of his garage, which was only a few steps away, and turned on the light — surely there was shelter there and the birds would be warm until morning.

But he soon discovered that there was a problem in communication. The birds did not respond to his shouted instructions, nor vigorous arm-waving, nor beckoning sweeps of a flashlight. They floundered helplessly about in the eddies of wind, with the light of the garage, had they but perceived it, only a few short yards away.

It dawned on the colonel then that God must have felt much the same, waving His arms, chiding His prophets, showing the way to an oblivious humanity. How easy it would all be, the colonel mused, if for only a few short moments I could be a bird and show the way. The holiday symbolized, after all, 'Immānū'ēl, God-with-us, the miracle of God made Man. The mission of the Redeemer is no more than God's subjective experience of the human plight — just long enough to show the way.

Jung himself found the antecedent to this epiphanous idea in the Book of Job. The point of this disquieting passion play is that God is not human, and "that is His greatness, that nothing human impinges on Him."[1] His infliction of terrible suffering on Job is neither innocent nor malevolent, but merely one facet of His bewildering in-humanity. The consequence of his troubling relationship with Job is a renewed interest in understanding Man from Man's viewpoint. The use of intermediaries, prophets given explicit instructions, has not produced results because of their infuriating *humanity*, which limits their empathic comprehension of the will of God. To accomplish the salvation of Mankind God must become Man, the Word becomes the flesh and spirit of Christ, the anointed Joshua; and through Christ's suffering not only are Man's sins relieved, but God is individuated![2] Being God is certainly a one-sided proposition (at least from the point of view of Job, as he morosely counts his losses and scratches

---

[1] Jung, *Memories, Dreams, Reflections*, p. 72.
[2] Jung, *Psychology and Religion: West and East*, p. 406.

his boils), and the experience of *being* Man as well as God is clearly a fulfilling transcendence.

Tolkien is a Christian theologian as well as literary demiurge, and he is particularly sensitive to this issue. The solution hit upon by the Guardians in their deliberations is nominally a Christian one, but commonly occurs in other religions. Even a particularly important link in our primate evolution was awarded a name suggestive of God's spirit incarnate.* None of the Valar may help Man without grasping his peculiar phenomenal outlook, without seeing life through human eyes. The only way to accomplish that without upsetting the development of history is to *be* Man.

Certain of the Maiar accepted incarnation in human form to aid in Middle-earth's battle with the forces of discord. These were the Istari, the Wise. Their form was human, as were their dispositions, and their powers were not those that they had possessed in holy form — only wisdom and understanding of at least that part of God's plan which had been revealed to the Guardians at the instant of creation. As Men they abandoned the raiment of the Holy Ones, the *fanar* or luminous veils worn by the Valar or Maiar when they appeared to Elves or Men. Each assumed a robe appropriate to his position in the Order. Only three are mentioned by name: Saruman, Gandalf, and Radagast.†

They combine elements of several important archetypes:

---

* *Ramapithecus: Rama* is very roughly the Hindu equivalent of Immanuel. The name suggests "ape-upon-whom-is-endowed-the-spirit-of-God." A look at reconstructions of this beauty convinces me that God must have, at least in our subjective god-image, a "Tookish part."
† Which has caused me to wonder from time to time what Radagast and his nameless brothers were doing while Saruman and Gandalf fought it out, considering the importance of the task. Radagast seems to have confined himself to ethology, a sort of epiphanous Konrad Lorenz; perhaps the other two were engaged in missionary work in Far Harad or east of the Plains of Rhûn.

Hero, Self, and Wise Old Man. They are by nature both personifying and transforming. In many ways they (especially Gandalf) are key symbols in the jigsaw puzzle of the psyche.

Gandalf was the Maia called Olórin, whose chief interest before assuming human form was the affairs of Middle-earth; Sauron was also a Maia with a similar hobby, but his own interests were hardly as benevolent. He was not, as we note in *The Fellowship of the Ring*, the chief of the Wise. This honor is at first clearly bestowed on Saruman, but Gandalf emerges finally as the chief wizard. This is a mystery neither *The Lord of the Rings* nor *The Silmarillion* explains. His eventual rise seems to have been preordained, since he of all the Wise is granted one of the Three, the Great Rings of the Elves. It is the gift of Círdan the Shipwright:

> For Círdan saw further and deeper than any other in Middle-earth, and he welcomed Mithrandir [Gandalf] at the Grey Havens, knowing whence he came and whither he would return.
>
> "Take this ring, Master," he said, "for your labours will be heavy; but it will support you in the weariness that you have taken upon yourself. For this is the Ring of Fire, and with it you may rekindle hearts in a world that grows chill. But as for me, my heart is with the Sea, and I shall dwell by the grey shores until the last ship sails. I will await you." [3]

Círdan is the guardian of the Grey Havens, the port of entry and exit in Middle-earth for those privileged to visit the Undying Lands. He is the boatman and guide of souls, the link (like Hermes, Anubis, and Charon) between life and death, West and East. If anyone knows who is who when the

[3] Tolkien, *The Lord of the Rings*, III: 332.

ships dock, it is he. The Ring of Fire, Rekindler, is not bestowed on any of the other Istari, even Saruman: "For Círdan saw further and deeper than any other . . ."

Gandalf's heroic qualities are abundantly outlined in all four books. His place is that of Redeemer, Rekindler of Hearts. This quality is reflected in his identification with the Third Ring, Narya, Ring of Fire. Fire is associated with cleansing, transformation (in the sense of alchemy), God, vigorous energy. The stone is red, symbolizing fire, passion, the sun, blood (and hence vigorous, "sanguinary" action), energy. Wherever Gandalf goes, hearts are strengthened, refreshed. Renewed spirit is in his wake; the decline of the West is slowed and halted by his presence.

This is only logical, since the West's travails are symbolically associated with Sauron, another Maia, whose evil influence has *sapped* the strength, resolve, and unity of Men and Elves. In Jungian theory, he is related to the ". . . mysterious and sinister Senex (Old Man),"[4] the counterpoint to the Promethean creativeness of Gandalf, whose variety of archetypal attributes includes heroism, wisdom, and shamanism (by virtue of his healing powers). The fall of Númenor was Sauron's doing, for he slyly poisoned the King's mind against mortality and the sacramental Valar. His lies and treachery have never been so evident as in the division of those who would oppose his will. He is the eternal enemy of creative synthesis, and being without honor himself he sows mistrust. As Gandalf is uniter and rekindler, Sauron is division and decay. The foes are well matched.

[4] Jung, *Mysterium Coniunctionis*, p. 87. At one point I had considered Saruman more closely identified with the principle of entropy (like Freud's Death instinct), in opposition to the quality of creative synthesis found in Gandalf's nature and role. Dr. Joseph L. Henderson, who consented to review the manuscript in draft, found this comparison questionable, and I was content to follow the suggestion of relationship to the Senex-figure in *Mysterium Coniunctionis*.

It is easy to personify Sauron as the shadow of Middle-earth, but he is really more complex than that. He is really all that can be unwholesome in both conscious and unconscious realms. His stronghold is the Land of Shadow, his symbol the fiery eye. The former is clearly associated with the unconscious, and the emotions at the source of that particular use of the imagery are entirely negative. Yet the fiery eye is closely akin to the common symbols of consciousness — in this context, the negative one-sided aspects of the conscious. Sauron is thus at once the one-sided neurotic consciousness and the dark and threatening shadow.

The "intent" of these symbols is thus shown to be less simple than meets the eye; for Gandalf combines elements of both conscious and unconscious by virtue of his ambiguous nature, and *his* symbol (the Ring of Fire) is a uniting one, a transcendental vision that heralds the coming of the Self rather than the pernicious one-sidedness of Red Eye and Shadow.

We should note the discussion in Chapter Two that deals with the two-sidedness of psychic energy — thoughts or emotions in the conscious sphere that have "opposite but equal" reactions in the unconscious. In this fashion the creation of positive images by the forces of light is twisted into grotesque parody by the forces of darkness. Elves taken by Morgoth are bred into hideous tribes of orcs, trolls are fashioned from dead stone "in mockery of ents"[5] formed from living wood.

Faërie itself is the embodiment of the creative aspects of both conscious and unconscious. The wholesome unconscious parts of Man lie to the West; the destructive, moribund beast of the unconscious lurks in the East. The one refreshes, binds together; the other tears asunder, decays.

[5] Tolkien, *The Lord of the Rings*, II: 77.

And both aspects, alas, are seen in the behavior of Man.

Tolkien seems to have glimpsed, as did Jung, this problem of modern Man. Tolkien chooses to personify this choice in the examples of Gandalf and Saruman. These two are similar enough to be brothers, and are members of the same order; yet under the dread of the East they follow different paths. Gandalf clings steadfastly to a union of the conscious glory of Númenor and the unconscious traditions of Faërie. Saruman rejects the West, the source of creativity, for what he perceives to be Man's destiny, but despite his cleverness lacks the wisdom to see that that destiny can never be fulfilled by rejecting its origins. Destiny is in union, not division.

Saruman begins the tale as "the White"; his color is not, as some may suppose, "no-color," but rather the subtractive sum of all colors (as the visible spectrum produces, when mixed, white light), and his original purpose on Middle-earth seems to have been one of uniting. Soon after the resumption of the narrative in *The Lord of the Rings*, however, he has found his uniting role dull, without intellectual challenge. His symbol is now disunion, as Gandalf soon sees:

> "I looked then and saw that his robes, which had seemed white, were not so, but were woven of all colours, and if he moved they shimmered and changed hue so that the eye was bewildered.
>
> " 'I liked white better,' I said.
>
> " 'White!' he sneered. 'It serves as a beginning. White cloth may be dyed. The white page can be overwritten; and the white light can be broken.'
>
> " 'In which case it is no longer white,' said I, 'and he that breaks a thing to find out what it is made of has left the path of wisdom.' "[6]

[6] Ibid., I: 248.

This is precisely the point that has eluded Saruman in his headlong Faustian embrace of conscious logic. White is the fusion of things and thus in the psychological sense not the beginning, but the final goal. The breaking up of the white is not a fresh start, but a regression.

This is the echo of the shattered nature of modern culture cited by Jung: the "sickness of dissociation" that afflicts human expression from religion to philosophy to art. The psychic fragmentation is due precisely to the denial of unconscious complexes. They cannot be shoved aside with adroit technology, nor successfully suppressed by the new mythology of science. This latter mythology is, of course, the one which "breaks a thing to find out what it is," and unless it retains the now dissected original's essence, it is an endeavor which had "left the path of wisdom." Goethe's Faust bemoans this spiritual inadequacy of reductionism as he comtemplates the years of study which have led him precisely nowhere:

> I have, alas, studied philosophy,
> Jurisprudence and medicine, too,
> And, worst of all, theology
> With keen endeavor, through and through —
> And here I am, for all my lore,
> The wretched fool I was before. [7]

A biology student may dissect the body of some unfortunate animal into heart, lungs, liver, etc.; but the parts displayed on the laboratory table are only parts, not the functioning unit. This is not an argument against scientific inquiry in general, nor against dissection; it is only a reminder that the whole of a pattern is always subtly greater

[7] Goethe, *Faust*, Pt I, ll. 354–59.

than the sum of its parts. This is what Saruman — and modern Man — discard in the inflation of the consciousness. The result is meaninglessness.

Saruman, like modern Man, delights in technology. His stronghold at Isengard is chock-full of gadgets — gears, chugs, clanks, and smells — much the same waste that Tolkien saw developing in his beloved Midlands. Interestingly, the only apparent purpose of all this machinery is to smell and pollute. Despite the obvious industry in the lower levels of Isengard, the hosts of Saruman still go to war with spear, arrow, and club. Perhaps it pleases the Crafty One simply to sit and watch his contraptions *run*, stroking the empty pride of his ego. Perhaps, on the other hand, Tolkien merely wanted to take a swipe at industrial waste. The landscape of Isengard is heavy industry in microcosm.

Saruman's plans for the Ring are in consonance with his thoroughly impoverished psychological set. Far from progress and growth, the Dark Lord of Mordor will simply be replaced by a Dark Lord of Isengard. In Saruman the negative aspects of the shadow are swollen beyond containing. Unable to find release in the symbols of the past, Saruman has put all his efforts into the future. But that future is only a fleeting shadow of greatness with no potential save spoilage.

Saruman's personality is *inflated*, swelled by the repression of unconscious material. The inflation of the ego may occur in two ways. In the most common, the ego may identify with its own persona (see Chapter Two and Figure 5), which is saying no more than that the ego foolishly believes its own propaganda. This is said to happen to politicians and generals.

The second cause of inflation is the ego's identification with an archetype of power. The conscious becomes for a time the "warlord" of its fate. This inflation might take the form of religious possession, identification with mythological themes (a pact with the devil, for instance), or similar outlets for energy-charged unconscious forces.

The specific case of Saruman is an example of identification with an archetype similar to that represented by Wotan (or Odin), the chief of the Norse/Teutonic gods, the *Aesir*. Jung chose this label for an archetype that he associated with wisdom, which is accompanied by darker impulses, daemonic possession. This is the wisdom and power of the sorcery represented by Sauron and his burgeoning disciple Saruman. Tolkien's probable identification of Sauron with Wotan has been suggested by other critics,[8] but what is important here is that Saruman's ego has identified with the terrible power of that figure, attempting to introject its power as an alternative to what seems to be hopeless opposition.*

This amplified power may have overtones of actual pathology or mental disturbance. The paranoid's delusions of grandeur may represent the distorted symbolization of such a powerful force intruding into the realm of consciousness. The entire personality is affected in the case of the paranoid form of schizophrenia — symptoms such as hallucinations, severely regressed behaviors, and other overt manifestations accompany the ascendent symptomatic theme of delusion. In the rather uncommon diagnosis of paranoia, however, the central delusion is stable, and other behaviors are no more unstable than anyone else's in a frequently insane world. In both cases the identification with unconscious forces has gone beyond dream and fanciful expression, and overridden the normal reality-testing function of the ego.

The forces surrounding this complex in Saruman's psyche

[8] Noel, *Mythology of Middle-earth*, p. 134–35.
* This may be an opening for an alternative Freudian interpretation, since identification is a necessary part of the resolution of the Oedipal conflict; the castration anxiety is relieved by mimicry of the loved and hated father. However, the story fails to suggest any logical mother image upon whom Saruman might cathect.

are overwhelming; the inflated consciousness, identified with Wotan, has dominated the ego's sphere of influence, and the result is a personality irresistibly tinged with shadow-themes.* When it becomes inescapably apparent that Saruman is beyond redemption, Gandalf must replace him in the symbolic structure. Presumably Círdan noted a flaw in Saruman's character when he passed the Ring of Fire to Mithrandir.

Gandalf, unlike Saruman, retains his ties with Faërie; he is still one of the Maiar despite his human incarnation. And it is not the mere mantle of humanity that brings about the downfall of Sauron or Saruman, since only the latter is incarnate. The seed of downfall is common to all kindreds, and regresses finally back to Melkor's original heresy before the creation. Gandalf sees this potential in himself (recognizes the negative aspects of his own shadow) when he vehemently refuses possession of the Ring. "Possession," he knows, is a word with ambivalent meaning where the Ring is concerned. The wholesome aspects of the unconscious (the West) win out in their battle with the negative aspects (the East).

No savior or redeemer walks the earth forever, and Gandalf is no exception. His years of human guise are tiring, filled with travel and care. And if the Valar are reluctant to meddle in the affairs of Middle-earth, there is another power at work. The Guardians do not control fate, though they have influenced it at critical moments. The master plan for all the kindreds originates in the thought of Ilúvatar, and in the

---

* The discerning reader should not make the mistake of interpreting this as the formation of a multiple personality, a type of hysterical dissociative neurosis; this is short of that dramatic reversal, the mere identification of the ego with some affect images, not a revolution. Nor is the character of Saruman "disordered" in the human, clinical sense; he is not human, merely a figure in Frodos Dreme.

complex tale of the War of the Ring there is the suggestion of this plan. This is not to suggest the absence of free will, for Man and Elf must both act *as if* they truly exercise it; and if this is the thought of The One made manifest in stimulus and response, and the concept of free will no more than a *post facto* label that Man in his hubris places on the ultimate causality, then there is still no debate. The *belief* in free will shapes the decisions made collectively and individually, whether they spring from some remote causality or not.

It is fated that Gandalf must replace Saruman, who has betrayed the trust of the Lords of the West. In so doing, Gandalf must undergo his own peculiar individuation and shed his mortal constraints.

The scene for this sudden change, like so many others, is in the dark places of the earth — the Mines of Moria. His confrontation with the unconscious allows the first full realization of the archetypal role of savior and redeemer. He literally sacrifices his life, or at least the earthly form of it, for the salvation of the Fellowship.

The Balrog — a literal "creature of shadow" — is his foe, a terrible demon of fire and darkness; and fittingly enough they battle for Middle-earth on a slender bridge. The dark caverns and halls through which the Fellowship has been pursued in its grope through the unconscious is connected with the world of light by the stone bridge, and Gandalf stands there, athwart the border of light and dark, to confront the personification of the shadow's terrible face. With the cracking of that bridge comes the severing of the epiphanous form of Gandalf the Grey. Together they fall into the deepest abyss of the earth, wizard and hopping-mad Balrog, reflecting the descent into the unconscious, into the dark pool of water, far out of sight and sound; the pool of inner wisdom, farthest regions of the collective unconscious. There the shadow's flames are quenched (his numen depotentiated). The upward movement — the long pursuit up the endless stair, like Jacob's ladder the bridge between heaven and earth — ends in a final battle on the platform next to the mountain's peak, in the full illumination of the sun. The shadow has been brought into the full light of consciousness and vanquished; and Gandalf is borne away in triumph by the eagle. His triumph is, as we shall see, bittersweet.

In this confrontation Gandalf is revealed for what he really is: "I am a servant of the Secret Fire, wielder of the Flame of Anor. You cannot pass. The dark fire will not avail you, flame of Udûn. Go back to the Shadow! You cannot pass."[9] The "secret fire" probably refers to the Flame Imperishable that is the visible form of the Song of the Ainur, the stuff of creation. That he is associated with it establishes his divine credentials. The Balrogs were once Maiar too, but like Sauron were seduced into the service of Melkor. "Flame of Udûn" refers to the valley that was the abode of the Balrogs in Elder Days. The probable intent here is to underscore the perversion of the Flame Imperishable.

The title "wielder of the Flame of Anor" is not quite as clear. The phrase seems to mean flame of the sun, but I find no reason to consider Gandalf a sun hero in the class of Mithras or Cúchulláinn. There is no mention of a deified sun in *The Silmarillion*, nor of an identity of the sun and the Flame Imperishable (the sun was a latecomer into the cosmos, as we have seen; the Eldar were born in the faint shimmer of starlight). The sun was, according to Tolkien's lore, formed of the fruit of Laurelin, one of the two trees of Valinor. The use of the word Anor (as in Minas Anor, Anárion, Anorien, etc.) as the personified sun may come from Anu, the sun-god of the Sumerians,[10] and it is possible that the real significance of this linguistic mess has eluded me — if

[9] Tolkien, *The Lord of the Rings*, I: 313.
[10] Hawkes, *Man and the Sun*, pp. 78–79.

indeed it exists at all. Perhaps this was just a detail of theology that Tolkien simply forgot to mention; but the flame is undeniably within the corporeal form of Gandalf.

When we see Gandalf next, he is Gandalf the White, body and raiment suffused with the *fana*, the glowing inner light of the Valar and Maiar. With the destruction of the Balrog and the literal death of Gandalf the greyness has been purged, and he has supplanted Saruman as the bearer of the Light of the West on earth. His own personal (but flawed) individuation is complete — as was God's in the Christian sense, by His completed experience in human form, which ends with the assumption of Christ.

He seems to be the same old Gandalf — a bit shaky still, like one who has been hit by a truck and survived — but despite the white beard and change of uniform he is recognizable as the wandering wizard. Yet there is something indefinable that has indeed changed. His strength is renewed, his endurance without limit: for in the shedding of all but the vestige of human form he is largely released from its physical limitations. He is refreshed, and the small and trivial experiences of Middle-earth move him again as in his youth in the West. Gone, too, are the hesitation and self-doubt that nearly claimed him on the bridge of Khazad-Dûm. Perhaps he has been granted a vision of the future, or maybe he just needed a slap in the face. In any case, he carries hope and renewed strength wherever he rides, and on the strength of his semidivine personality must rest the hopes for the Self-realization of Middle-earth.*

Gandalf's aspects are both personifying and transforming. In his role as the physical embodiment of both Faërie and

* The Christian analogy of this brief and inspiring interregnum is the period described in the gospels between the resurrection and the assumption. I am inclined to believe that Tolkien's intent here was explicitly a reference to Christ.

Middle-earth (Maia and Man, God and Man) he is the union of opposites. In his opposition to Saruman is the conscious fulfillment of the archetype of the Hostile Brethren, often cited as an early phase of the hero myth. With the resolution of this initial strife (the decline of Saruman and the supremacy of Gandalf) the division between conscious and unconscious is partially resolved. Gandalf is thus transformed into a personification of the "superior" man in a variety of key roles: first the transformer, then the initiated one who carries the power of healing and redemption. All this is in harmony with the growing realization of the Self.*

For his part in binding the dissociation of Middle-earth (the most trying part of his feat is the refusal of the Ring) Gandalf remains in the realm of Men only a short time; he must return to the Grey Havens, thence to the West. Saruman has failed the test and at the point of death his human shell shrivels; his tired spirit is refused by the West, to drift away on the wind a homeless, bitter wraith. There should be a lesson here, and we will deal with it in a later chapter.

Gandalf's second symbolic function is that of guide, the hermeneut. We have examined this archetypal theme earlier, and noted its peculiar etymology, the identification of the Greek god Hermes with the guiding function. He is the conductor of dead souls from the land of the living to the underworld, and his sacred phallic image, the herm, was set at crossroads for this reason.[11] The form is phallic, as we have seen earlier, because of its suggestion of the union between light and dark, male and female — the *coincidentia oppositorum;* the wizard's staff, too, contains this image, both because of transcendence and the idea of literal potency. This

---

* For this analysis of the symbolic role of Saruman and Gandalf I am indebted to Joseph Henderson.

[11] Henderson, "Ancient Myths and Modern Man" in *Man and His Symbols*, ed. C. G. Jung, p. 155.

was a principal function assigned to the Wise — to guide rather than to confront the Dark Lord in person for reasons of caution. Radagast, the third wizard, bears the name of a Russian nature-god associated with Hermes,[12] and I must conclude that the hermeneutic role was the one intended by Tolkien for the Istari.

A question that might be fairly asked here is why, given Tolkien's apparent intent to interject the themes of Christian theology into his fantasy, the analogy of God-made-man is not more direct. Why did the King of the Valar (Manwë) or Ilúvatar Himself not assume human form, rather than a mere team of lesser Guardians? Surely there would have been one or more of the lordly Valar, at least — Aulë the smith or Oromë the swift hunter — who would undertake the task.

I must admit that I am not entirely satisfied with the answer, which presumes that the form of myth is more rigidly subservient to Jungian dynamics than most critics would accept, or, alternatively, that Tolkien was consciously determined to make the story fit the psychological predispositions. If the former is true, then the theme of realization of the Self is powerful enough to have dominated entirely a most vital part of *The Lord of the Rings*.

In theory, an approach to the archetypes is carried by the anima or animus as "spirit-guide," personified as a woman for men (and a man for women). Tolkien does not appear to have been entirely comfortable with the females in his myth. His only feminine characterizations were either androgynous (Galadriel and the formidable Wagnerian Éowyn) or self-consciously stereotypic (Mrs. Maggot, Rosie Cotton, Arwen Undómiel), flighty or submissive enough to suit the fantasies of any male chauvinist.

The sole exception — and the only acceptable anima figure at the higher level (we will examine Frodo's specific

[12] Noel, *Mythology of Middle-earth*, p. 188.

anima later) — is Varda, spouse of the Elder King. There is no hint in *The Lord of the Rings* or in *The Silmarillion* of any wifely subservience; in fact, the superficial designation of masculinity or feminity to the Ainur (Valar) was an arbitrary assessment of the overall tone of the deities' respective personae. They called the one the figurative spouse of the other, but this only suggests that they kept frequent company rather than suffering the addition of sex to gender. They certainly did not *breed* — their creative conceptions were altogether immaculate. Nevertheless, these figures are the stuff of animae(i).

Given this framework, step back now from the profusion of trees and try to take in the forest! If we organize the whole of Tolkien's world, including hints of the physical geography of the Undying Lands, and reduce them to a very general map, we begin to glimpse —as we might expect — an odd and compelling symmetry. It is reminiscent of the Taoist concept of reintegration of the soul's disparate parts after death. The spirit of Man divides into yin and yang, the male and female principles. They are personified as "Mistress of the West" and "Lord of the East" (the latter identified with the "Dark City").[13] This is the perfect mythic analogy to our present union of opposites. The male and female union is balanced and compensatory on two different levels. Jung describes in a piece of his own active imagination that a Gnostic philosopher, Basilides, in *Septem Sermones ad Mortuos*, pronounces the following:

> Spirituality conceiveth and embraceth. It is womanlike and therefore we call it MATER COELESTIS, the celestial mother. Sexuality engendereth and createth. It is manlike, and therefore we call it PHALLOS, the earthly father.
>
> The sexuality of man is more of the earth, the sexuality of woman is more of the spirit.

[13] Franz, *C. G. Jung: His Myth in Our Time*, p. 286.

> The spirituality of man is more of the heaven, it goeth to the greater.
>
> The spirituality of woman is more of the earth, it goeth to the smaller.
>
> . . . .
>
> Each must go to its own place.[14]

The White Lady faces the Dark Lord, each gazes out from his own high place.

The White Lady's abode is on the twin peaks of Fanuilos, the white mountain of the Uttermost West, in the domed hall of Oromardi; this high place is shared with her spouse, Manwë the Elder King. But his gaze is not directed at Middle-earth, and we must conclude that it is directed instead outward, toward the heavens. She diverts her attention and power toward Middle-earth, through the Pass of Calacirya in the encircling mountains. She is the feminine symbol, distillation of what is benevolent in the divinity, and she is clothed in pure white light.[15] Her remote vantage is encircled in white cloud, her celestial companion is the setting sun.

The Dark Lord's stronghold is the Dark Tower of Barad-Dûr, in the dead land of Mordor; he shares his abode with no

[14] Jung, "Sermo V", *VII Sermones ad Mortuos*, p. 27.
[15] Tolkien and Swann, *The Road Goes Ever On*, p. 67.

FIGURE 11. WHITE LADY, DARK LORD

In this stylized representation of Tolkien's World, the dichotomous nature of physical geography is strikingly apparent. The feminine West, Faërie, is personified as Varda, enthroned on the far distant white peak; the brilliant light that characterizes Her appearance to Men and Elves, streamed through the pass of Calacirya ("light-cleft") toward Middle-earth across the sundering seas. The masculine East is symbolized by the Dark Lord on his dark throne in Barad-Dûr; balanced against the light of the West (albedo) is the dark cloud of Orodruin (negredo) that pours over the Vale of Sorcery (Imlad Morgul).

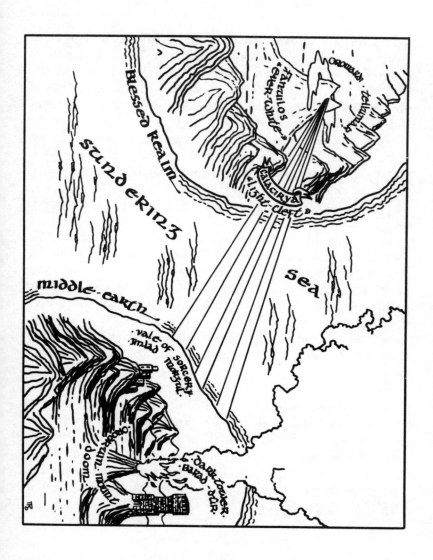

spouse but the dreadful female spider Shelob, daughter of Morgoth's pet Ungoliant from the Elder Days. His gaze is directed to the West in bitterness, with envy and malice laden beyond comprehension, through Cirith Ungol, Pass of the Spider, and the Valley of Sorcery, peopled with wraiths and foul things as the Pass of Calacirya is inhabited by the fair Elves of the West. He is the masculine symbol, the essence of evil, and he is clothed in darkness. *His* fastness is wreathed in black, sooty cloud, his symbol in the heavens is the rising moon.

They are separated by the sundering seas, but their gaze is ever directed across it.

These are the parallels; we might hastily conclude that they are mirror images of one another. But this is not so. The important contrast is in the union of opposites that characterizes each. The Elder King and Queen together make up a differentiated whole, MATER COELESTIS and PHALLOS; a conjunction which is wholesome. The Dark Lord is undifferentiated, an inflated shadow figure without psychic compensation. The balancing feminine is Shelob, an entirely negative power.

The feminine energy of the White Lady was extremely influential among the High Elves (those who had once dwelt in the Undying Lands and knew her firsthand). They called her Star-Queen, Kindler of Stars (Elbereth Gilthoniel).[16] Their prayers were directed to her, not Manwë, as befits her role as Queen of the unconscious. Her very name is a talisman of power, as in Sam's spontaneous, almost glossolalic chant in *Lord of the Rings*, II: 301.

> *O! Queen who kindled star on star,*
> *White-robed from heaven gazing far,*

---

[16] Tolkien and Swann, *The Road Goes Ever On*, p. 72.

> *Here overwhelmed in dread of Death*
> *I cry: O guard me, Elbereth!* [17]

The chant suggested in *The Lord of the Rings*, I: 228, identical in meter but less urgent in tone, is similar to an invocation translated in full by Tolkien in later expansion:

> O! Elbereth who lit the stars, from glittering crystal slanting falls with light like jewels from heaven on high the glory of the starry host. To lands remote I have looked afar, and now to thee, Fanuilos, bright spirit clothed in ever-white,* I here will sing beyond the Sea, beyond the wide and sundering Sea. [18]

which, although perfectly acceptable at face value as a reverential hymn to a feminine deity, also has significance as a wish for conscious personification of the anima-archetype — the necessary prelude to Self-realization.

Varda's connection with symbols of the Self is strongly suggested by special aspects of the chant cited above: '. . . from glittering crystal slanting falls with light like jewels from heaven on high the glory of the starry host." Tolkien reveals that "*silivren* (white) glittering would recall to Elvish minds the *silmarils* and describe the stars as crystalline forms shining from within with a light of mysterious power." He adds: "Both *silivren* and *silma-ril* contain the name *silima* that Fëanor gave the crystal substance he devised and alone could

---

[17] This translation of the Elvish verse in *The Lord of the Rings* is found in Tolkien and Swann, *The Road Goes Ever On*, p. 72.
* The literal meaning of *Fanuilos* is apparently "Mount Ever-white" (Cf. Barad-Dûr, "Dark Tower"); this is apparently a metaphorical mind's-eye vision of Varda as the High Elves beheld her back in the Good Old Days, her form identified with her distant mountain dwelling.
[18] Ibid.

make."[19] This reference to the crystal form and the specific symbolic function of the silmarils has been discussed earlier; Tolkien uses the crystal frequently as a symbolic motif, always in the context of perfection, union, renewal. The "glittering crystal" stars kindled by Varda are thus essentially one with the Arkenstone of Thrain, the jewels of the Three Rings, the Elf-stone Elessar, the *palantíri*, and the silmarils.

It may be facile to explain away this personality, apparently quite inessential to the story, as a "mere" reference to the Blessed Virgin (at least as much so as calling *lembas* a reference to the Holy Wafer). She may be just that. Tolkien certainly visualizes her as intermediary, in the sense of the Deified Mary's role in the Roman Church. It is she of whom the Elves beg grace: "She was often thought of, or depicted as, standing on a great height looking towards Middle-earth, with eyes that penetrated the shadows, and listening to the cries for aid of Elves (and Men) in peril or grief. Frodo . . . and Sam both invoke her in moments of extreme peril. The Elves sing hymns to her. (This and other references to religion in *The Lord of the Rings* are often overlooked.)"[20] But there have always been religious expressions of the female side of God's (and Man's) nature, as Tolkien was aware. Varda may fulfill this potential at a deeper level, a White Goddess from the dawn of human thought, just as *lembas* may refer to a concept of transformation of far remoter antiquity than the Eucharist.

Whether or not I am on firm ground is, like most of the assertions in this discussion, debatable; however, precedents for this kind of theme are not unknown. In *The White Goddess*, his abstruse investigation of poetic device, Robert Graves

---

[19] Tolkien and Swann, *The Road Goes Ever On*, p. 73.
[20] Ibid.

cites the following verse associated with a pre-Christian cult of Hercules:

> *Seek the Lord, the beloved of the Great Goddess.*
> *When he is borne ashore, you shall find him.*
> *When he performs great feats, you shall wonder.*
> *When he reigns, you shall share his glory.*
> *When he rests, you shall have repose.*
> *When he departs, you shall go with him*
> *To the Western Isle, paradise of the blest.*[21]

Graves presents this verse as evidence of the debt of early Christianity to a pagan poetic and mythic lore. My heart leaped when I first saw these lines, which hardly demand much elaboration to show their relevance to the story of Gandalf. My fingers itched to type, in capitals, QUOD ERAT DEMONSTRANDUM. But it does not offer any more than a slender support to my speculations on the reluctance of God to appear in the flesh.

In any case, it is unlikely that Manwë will descend from his throne as a human; Varda, his snowy spouse, is the one who keeps an eye out for the fortunes of Elf and Man. Varda befits an anima-figure who is out of place in the conscious world of men. Presumably the other Valar were tired of the whole business after ages of contending with Melkor's outrages (and after the regrettable unpleasantness with Ar-Pharazôn). Remember, also, that the wrath of the Valar in Elder Days twice caused the devastation of vast tracts of land, for which reason the Guardians long forbore direct military action; perhaps they were not enthusiastic over the prospects of destroying Middle-earth in order to save it. So the Maiar drew the detail.

---

[21] Graves, *The White Goddess*, p. 423.

I am not convinced, but this explanation such as it is will have to do. Since this is after all only a fairy tale — only a fairy tale! — it is not necessary to make all the pieces fit. Even dreams are hard to pin down. But the subcreator is so meticulous in exploring the wealth of mythic image that a great many of the universal patterns of affect and power must emerge from his work. Elbereth will have to do as the prime mover.*

* An interesting counterpoint to the figure of Varda is in C. S. Lewis' attempt at lay theology for children, *The Lion, the Witch, and the Wardrobe,* where the White Witch provides a good example of the characterization of the negative anima in literature. Why the projections of the eternal feminine in these two friends took such contrasting forms would be an interesting matter of speculation; Lewis married quite late in life, while Tolkien maintained a devotion to wife and hearth outside the borders of the Eagle and Child.

Tolkien, incidentally, was not reluctant to deal with the Elder King; *Smith of Wootton Major* tells in part of the King of Faërie's incarnate amusements.

VII
trickster, tree, and terminal man

SIMILARITY in plot and symbol between *The Hobbit* and *The Lord of the Rings* has been discussed in an earlier chapter. The likenesses are only natural, since both works tell the same story, and in many particulars employ the same cast of characters. Some of these superficial parallels are worth a closer examination because of their revealing hidden contrasts. Bilbo and Frodo are clearly cast from different molds despite their origins — Bilbo is from beginning to end the well-to-do rustic gentlehobbit who gains in erudition and finds Self "under hill and over hill"; and Frodo is the chosen savior of Middle-earth, lacking his uncle's cheerful yeoman pluck and eternal fussy optimism. Gandalf is really three characters: the slightly comical wandering conjuror of *The Hobbit*, the grumpy careworn crusader of pre-Balrog pages in *The Lord of the Rings,* and the reborn Maia, suffused with the inner light of the Holy Ones. The nature of the quest is changed, made more grave and universal in the later work, although the overall resolution is the same. But the most fruitful comparisons are often to be made among the "lesser" characters. The most memorable of these are Beorn the skin-changer, the elusive Tom Bombadil, and the stately Tree-beard.

Tolkien does not provide the slightest clue as to the origin of Beorn or Bombadil in the appendices or *The Silmarillion*. This is odd in itself, as the places of so many creatures are carefully set down and fitted meticulously into the plan of subcreation. The pedigree of the Balrogs is pretty clear; there are educated speculations on the origins of orc and troll, and the ents have their own footnote in the tale of the demiurgic labors of the Valar. Beorn and Bombadil lie outside this greater internally consistent framework. Yet the evocative power of these figures — particularly Bombadil — is clear to the reader, even when the interludes in the house of Beorn and the house of Bombadil are seemingly no more than puzzling interruptions, inessential to the final resolution of the high and serious issues. The reasons for their insertion into the story become clearer, however, when they are viewed in Jungian perspective.

BEORN

Beorn is represented as a tall, powerful, ageless man; a mysterious grumpy recluse. He is, moreover, no ordinary man, but a "skin-changer," who can assume the form of a giant bear at will, fierce and vindictive in dealing with foes, chiefly orcs. He speaks the tongues of animals, and his servants are magical dogs and horses whose company he obviously values more than that of other, lesser men. Tolkien speculates that he might have been a bear of the Misty Mountains who could take human form,[1] but Beorn's offspring, the Beornings, are

---

[1] Tolkien, *The Hobbit*, pp. 116–17.

men, so we must conclude (as Tolkien seems to have done) that the bearded hermit is human.*

Beorn's nature is dual: he is both man and beast, reflecting the dual nature of the psyche. He is at ease with both aspects. The fusion of these opposite but happily congruent qualities is suggestive of the transcendental function of the Self. Von Franz notes that:

> The Self is often symbolized as an animal, representing our instinctive nature and its connectedness with one's sur-roundings. (That is why there are so many helpful animals in myths and fairy tales.) The relation of the Self to all the surrounding nature and even to the cosmos probably comes from the fact that the "nuclear atom" of our psyche is somehow woven into the whole world, both inner and outer.[2]

The position of animals in harmony with nature is the wonder and envy of Man, for it is precisely this harmony that Man has lost by repudiating his animal origins to feed the conceit of his conscious humanness. The remnants of this longing for unity with nature, the lost Eden of Man's phy-logenetic heritage, are to be found in such figures of fancy. Beorn's role as helper and guide, and his ancestry, is in the primitive human condition:

> In ways that are still completely beyond our comprehen-sion, our unconscious is . . . attuned to our surround-ings — to our group, to society in general, and, beyond these, to the whole of nature. Thus The Great Man of the

---

* This has always interested me, being like Genesis curiously uninformative on certain key issues: e.g., who was *Mrs*. Beorn?

[2] Franz, "The Process of Individuation" in *Man and His Symbols*, ed. C. G. Jung, p. 207.

Naskapi Indians does not merely reveal inner truths; he also gives hints about when and where to hunt. And so from dreams of the Naskapi hunter evolve the words and melodies of the magical songs with which he attracts the animals.[3]

Beorn is entirely at one with his evolutionary heritage, a shamanistic hermit with the soul of a bear. He is totally above deceit (since deceit is above all a plaything of the conscious), and so seemingly immune to deception.[*] The petty concerns of conscious man are of no import to him unless they intrude on the grumpy solitude of his house; of these disturbances of the peace he is most intolerant, a berserker, terrifying avenger as incapable of human mercy as he is of human evil.

We may place Beorn in the general category of Self symbols because of his symbolic hermaphrodism (not in the sexual sense, of course, but in the more global concept of union of opposites), and the position he occupies is the transcender of Man and animal, conscious and unconscious, thought and instinct. As with many such collective images, he assumes a second role: the guide. He is particularly suited to this role because of his innocence of conscious bias. He is, as Gandalf suggests, "under no enchantment but his own."[4]

But his grounding is in the unconscious; and despite his human form, it is in the darker unconscious realm that his power originates. He is the shadow of Man without the taint of consciousness gone wrong, and an illustration of the folly

[3] Franz, "The Process of Individuation" in *Man and His Symbols*, ed. C. G. Jung, p. 208.
[*] This is a notion that Tolkien pursues still further, not only in the characterization of Bombadil but also in the nature of the noble barbarians of Rohan — who are, interestingly enough, described in the appendices as akin to the Beornings.
[4] Tolkien, *The Hobbit*, p. 116.

of personifying that complex as the frightful fiend. Jung takes care to point out that:

> If the repressed tendencies . . . were obviously evil, there would be no problem whatever [in vanquishing and breaking up the shadow as a part of Self-realization]. But the shadow is merely . . . primitive, unadaptive and awkward; not wholly bad. It even contains childish or primitive qualities which would in a way vitalize and embellish the human existence. . . .[5]

The choice of the bear as the animal symbol is a careful one, and very much in consonance with Tolkien's heavy reliance on the mythic themes of Northern Europe. The bear was revered by the Celts, and the form of the she-bear was often used as a pictorial convention for the Great Goddess; the dream representation of the bear as a symbolic theme is not infrequently bisexual (as the union of opposites).[6] Norse and Teutonic myth enoble the bear, and the personification of the beast aspect of Man is one aspect of this metaphor — the Norse *berserks* (Ruth Noel suggests, after Grimm, that the term originally meant "bear-shirt"[7]) were literally bears in their archetypal rage. Beorn's personality is certainly ursine: like that animal he is hairy, powerful, crotchety, and fatuous. Gandalf cautions Bilbo that Beorn is not a fellow to be trifled with: "You must be careful not to annoy him, or heaven knows what will happen. He can be appalling when he is angry, though he is kind enough when humored."[8] (Read: "stay inside the car and take pictures; do NOT stick

[5] Jung, *Psychology and Religion: West and East*, p. 78.
[6] Noel, *Mythology of Middle-earth*, p. 91.
[7] Ibid.
[8] Tolkien, *The Hobbit*, p. 116.

your hand out the window.") His very name means "bear."[9]

Primitive tribes (and not so primitive ones as well) often identify their individual and collective souls with the projections of animals of this totemic sort. Freud made much of this as evidence of the Primal Horde experience[*] and the cultural pervasiveness of the incest taboo,[10] but Jung suggests that this hypothesis misses a deeper psychological significance. Shamanistic assumption of animal virtues (and sometimes costume and behavior) is often a central feature of ritual. The Roman standard-bearer wore the skins of wolves or bears as a badge of rank even in the most cynical of centuries; and the burden of the *Aquilifer* was a gilded eagle, symbol of Juppiter Optimus Maximus, and the legionary deity. The numinous quality of these identifying theriomorphic ("beast-form") symbols is even apparent in the assumption of animal names by athletic teams and Boy Scout troops![†]

The association of hero myths and animal qualities has been noted by analytical psychologists. The stages in devel-

---

[9] Noel, *Mythology of Middle-earth*, p. 178.

[*] This refers to the theory that forms the basis of a phylogenetic explanation of castration anxiety, which Freud extracted from Darwin, Lamarck, and case studies. The primordial father was a strong patriarchal figure (like the leader of a baboon horde) who preserved peace in the hunter-gatherer family group by driving out the male children when they reached puberty. (A more contemporary ritual enactment is in the pubertal circumcision and "walkabout" — probably, given the nature of the ceremony, more of a "limpabout" — of aboriginal tribes in Australia.) According to Freud's interpretation, a group of sons so disenfranchised banded together and returned to kill and devour the father. Their second thoughts, which dwelt at least partly on the observation that a bad precedent had been set, led to the first step toward social order — the incest taboo. In Freud's view, this was the first faltering step in the direction of organized society.

[10] See Freud, *Totem and Taboo*.

[†] And in Sherif and Sherif's classic study in social psychology at Robber's Cave, in which groups of boys in summer camp identified so strongly with their totem figures — Eagles and Rattlers — that they almost came to

opment of the hero parallel the development of the psyche from birth to death. Joseph L. Henderson suggests that:

> . . . It is essential to recognize that in each of the stages in this cycle there are special forms of the hero story that apply to the particular point reached by the individual in the development of his ego-consciousness, and to the specific problem confronting him at that moment. That is to say, the image of the hero evolves in a manner that reflects each stage of the evolution of the human personality.[11]

The most primitive form has been called the Trickster.* He is "a figure whose physical appetites dominate his behavior; he has the mentality of an infant.[12] Henderson uses the examples of the Chinese dramatic figure Monkey and Charlie Chaplin in *Modern Times;* I suggested once in a course on the personality of black Americans that Br'er Rabbit fit this mold in America's hybrid folklore.† Next on the level of development is the Hare, who also commonly assumes animal form, but emerges as the transforming founder of the culture, often its savior.[13] Quetzalcoatl and the totem-hero Raven of the Pacific Northwest Amerindian culture fall roughly into this category. Beorn has clearly outgrown the pure physical appetites of Trickster, but is hardly a socialized being; his interpretation of the Self is still primitive,

---

blows and provided a landmark demonstration of in-group out-group phenomenon. (Cf. Sherif and Sherif, *An Outline of Social Psychology*, p. 69.)

[11] Henderson, "Ancient Myths and Modern Man" in *Man and His Symbols*, ed. C. G. Jung, p. 112.

* The names have been drawn from the myth cycle of the Amerindian Winnebago tribe.

[12] Ibid.

† The durability of these personifications is quite striking: compare the story of Br'er Sparrow with the ghetto poem "The Signifyin' Monkey."

[13] Ibid., p. 113.

grounded in instinctual expression rather than conscious so-phistication.

His appearance in *The Hobbit* follows Bilbo's first glimpse of the quality of untamed libido that resides in his own un-conscious (trolls) and the first foray into that realm, when he first confronts elements of his shadow complex (Gollum). These experiences launch him on his dream search for the Self, and his first experience of the transforming savior-hero personification of that goal is naturally primitive and un-developed, the bear-man. It remains for Bard the Bowman to be the final, fully realized hero, whose emergence parallels Bilbo's own figurative rebirth.

Frodo, too, must confront the primitive hero and guide, the symbolic heir to the sketchily developed Beorn: the haunting, enigmatic forest-master Tom Bombadil.

OLD TOM

Tom Bombadil combines elements of several archetypes, and his place on the map of Middle-earth that has eluded critics and investigators is more clearly established when we dis-cover his position on the map of the psyche; for he stands squarely athwart the path to the Self. His origin is unknown even to Elrond and the Wise: "Oldest-and-Fatherless" he was called in Elder Days, Iarwain Ben-adar. We are told that his various names mean "old," and "sorcery," "very old, origi-nal." His claim as the oldest of Middle-earth's inhabitants is contested, seemingly, by the ents. This is curious, since Tol-kien was quite meticulous in his establishment of internal consistency, and this conflict is entirely uncharacteristic of the orderly cross-referencing of the rest of the books. I think, however, that there is actually no conflict, and that this ap-parent impossibility is the real key to Bombadil's nature and origins.

A common and potent archetype is Original Man, which

Jung often calls Anthropos, emerging as a conscious representative of the Self. Bombadil, despite his apparently humble digs in the Old Forest, is the prototype of the Children of God, that Original Man and the template which will influence the final form of Man. That he is at least as old as Middle-earth itself he willingly admits: "Mark my words, my friends: Tom was here before the river and the trees; Tom remembers the first raindrops and the first acorn."[14] In fact, he predates Middle-earth, and is the cosmic seed from which Man develops.

The creation of the world from the void was through the Song of the Ainur, the divine refrain taught to the Holy Ones by Ilúvatar before the beginning of days. In those tunes of glory were contained the form and history of the world and of the Children of God. The *Ainulindalë* was transformed into light, the light into matter, and through this device The One revealed to them their handiwork. Yet the entire story, the final telling of the tale, was not revealed to the demiurgic Valar; only a partial vision was granted, and the creation of His children and their final doom is in the hands of The One. The Valar will only prepare the Realm, act as stewards in His stead.

The tireless Ruth Noel informs us that "Bombadil" is derived from the Middle-English words for "humming" and "hidden."[15] This is his name; by the Elves he is called Oldest-and-Fatherless, "Old Sorcerer" by the Dwarves, "Ancient" by Men. Yet his origin and essence are contained only in Bombadil, his own name for himself, for its meaning is known only to him and his inventor:

> "Who are you, Master?" he [Frodo] asked.
> "Eh, what?" said Tom sitting up, and his eyes glinting

[14] Tolkien, *The Lord of the Rings*, I: 132.
[15] Noel, *Mythology of Middle-earth*, p. 128.

in the gloom. "Don't you know my name yet? That's the only answer."[16]

And in truth it is the only answer. The form of the *Ainulindalë*, the song of the Holy Ones who were the offspring of the thought of Ilúvatar, and from whom they learned their songs, was wordless, pure tone, ages from creative articulation. Interwoven with the melody were all the creations, including Man and Elf. Old Tom is, I venture to speculate, the "hidden melody," the secret tune of The One from which His children took form and grew, the divine tonal DNA! His songs are, after all, "stronger songs."*

This interpretation gives even greater significance to Tom's immunity from the effects of the Ring. The daemonic power of the Ring derives from the personification of discord that was Melkor. Melkor was, as we have seen, the Ainu whose fierce pride and stubborn individuality brought evil into the world; and he was cast, Lucifer-like, into the void at the end of the First Age. This tradition of mayhem was carried on by the fallen Maia Sauron, the greater part of whose power was invested in the Ring — a power which derived originally from Melkor. But the song that is the genesis of Bombadil is that strain which was untouched by Melkor, the promise of Ilúvatar to His children; and in this fashion the Ring's power has no way of affecting him. This is also Man's hope.

Since Tom is the Original Man, conceived as both alpha

[16] Tolkien, *The Lord of the Rings*, I: 132.
* The name Bombadil may, I add in all fairness, have no such etymological connotation, but may be merely a child's nonsense word which crept informally into print; see Carpenter, *J. R. R. Tolkien*, p. 165. If the name was coincidental, it was attached to a character who was certainly not — Tolkien was anything but whimsical about whimsy. The prototype of Bombadil as the magic song-master was probably the Finnish hero Lemminkainen in the *Kalevala*.

and omega of Man's development, he also represents a sort of innate, predestined goal — the personification, if you will, of the genetic potential, or Self-actualization. It is this characteristic that most unambiguously defines him as the manifestation of the Self archetype, albeit a primitive one. This is an enchanting vision of Man's destiny: rugged individualists romping about the shores of private Waldens, singing to trees and dining on bread and honey. Certainly Old Tom is a Self-realized being, "his own master," for whom the magnet of incongruence has no fatal attraction. Glorfindel prophesies at the Council of Elrond that in the darkest hour Bombadil would succumb, last as he was first. But Old Tom's songs are literally stronger than Hell, and we might suspect that he is less worried than the Wise for knowing how the songs will end.

Tom's role is hermeneutic; he gives guidance to Frodo after his fashion (which is very "nondirective," as a Rogerian might say) and offers a haven and a charm for protection. Yet his advice is not the same as Gandalf's or Aragorn's; it is the stuff of riddles. His affairs are not those of the Third Age or any other age, and his memory stretches back before the birth of Elves and Men to the time when a new world lay silently under the twinkling light of stars; and his vision stretches forward to the end of days.

His stage of development in the myth cycle, at least to the extent that his peculiar personality is perceived by lesser beings, is ambiguous. To the rural hobbits of Buckland and the Marish he is Trickster, as is clearly demonstrated in "The Adventures of Tom Bombadil." This comic poem, along with "Bombadil Goes Boating," is offered by Tolkien as a local legend of the eastern Shire set in verse. The degree of sophistication of the hero's image is delineated by the sophistication of the culture that experiences him. The Bucklanders' assessment of Bombadil is described as befits the

Trickster: "Mysterious maybe and unpredictable but none-theless comic."[17] His legendary skills include the speech of animal and vegetable, but he is not associated with any beast in the totemic sense; he is consistently the human blueprint.

But Bombadil is a male figure without a hint of androgyny. His speech, a dizzy blank verse full of nonsense and neologistic word-salad, contains no identifiable feminine aspects. This renders him symbolically incomplete and thus a less than adequate representation of the Self. For this reason he is provided a consort, his anima personified and tamed. Goldberry is the water made flesh as Bombadil is of the earth. Together they are *Phallos* and *Mater Coelestis*. She is passive and reflective, he never slows down or shuts up. After a winter of Tom's constant bustle and blither she gratefully takes her annual vacation to the quiet shores of the Withywindle! But they make the most stable of pairs, warp and weft of the *mysterium coniunctionis;* they are the perfect whole, personification of the principle of equivalence. They are complementary and compensating, as the amused hobbits discern:

> . . . The hobbits sat half in wonder and half in laughter: so fair was the grace of Goldberry and so merry and odd the caperings of Tom. Yet in some fashion they seemed to weave a single dance, neither hindering the other, in and out of the room, and round about the table . . .[18]

Even without benefit of clergy, they are yin and yang.

This suggests a more complex meaning to the union of Tom and Goldberry. The courtship, if that is what that gentle abduction could be called, is a miniature individuation in itself. Goldberry is the River-woman's daughter, and lives

[17] Tolkien, *The Adventures of Tom Bombadil*, p. 81.
[18] Tolkien, *The Lord of the Rings*, I: 132.

under the surface of the Withywindle — that is, in the unconscious. This special wedding is a repetition of the theme of the *coniunctio:* this role of the anima is as the female part of the psyche wedded (in the unconscious) to the male, completing the whole. The theme is repeated yearly and takes on the additional ordered meaning of the seasons personified.

This is the crux of Tom's hermeneutic function: the duty to show the way. Since he is both original and "terminal" Man, his example alone is a powerful impetus and a haunting one, else many a reader would have viewed the hiatus in the Old Forest as nothing more than the resident whimsicality in what Edmund Wilson called a fairy story "somehow out of hand."[19]

TREEBEARD

The ents were created as an accident of history. One of the Valar had supervised the careful ordering of trees; her spouse was the teacher of the Elves, and equipped them with the means and the skills to hew wood for their legitimate purposes. This started a divine squabble, which ended in a gentle compromise: the creation of the Onodrim, shepherds of trees who would cherish and protect their leafy look-alikes.[20]

The tree is a frequent symbol in dream, myth, and religion. In these one-sided days we seldom pause to contemplate the significance of the ill-favored, amputated evergreens on sale during the Christmas holidays, but their persistence as part of the celebration of Christ's birth and Man's salvation is evidence enough of the power of this notion. Jung described a particularly intense dream — the earliest he could remember, sometime between his third and

[19] Wilson, "Oo, Those Awful Orcs!" *The Nation* (April 14, 1956).
[20] Tolkien, *The Silmarillion*, p. 53.

fourth years — of an underground temple in which was enthroned a gigantic phallic tree which (according to his later interpretation) symbolized a variety of abstruse dimensions of his early ambivalent views of religion.[21] In his own contributions to *Man and His Symbols* Jung suggests that:

> A tree is one of the best examples of a motif that often appears in dreams (and elsewhere) and that can have an incredible variety of meanings. It might symbolize evolution, physical growth, or psychological maturation; it might symbolize sacrifice or death (Christ's crucifixion on the tree); it might be a phallic symbol; it might be a great deal more.[22]

And Joseph Henderson adds in the same work:

> We know from many examples that an ancient tree or plant represents symbolically the growth and development of psychic life (as distinct from instinctual life, commonly symbolized by animals).[23]

The tree may also symbolize, more explicitly, Man's development: "The tree is as it were an intermediate form of man . . ."[24] It is also connected with individuation, as Jung described in a case study concerning

> . . . a schizophrenic patient in whose cosmic system the Father-God had a tree growing out of his breast. It bore red and white fruits, or spheres, which were worlds. Red

[21] Jung, *Memories, Dreams, Reflections*, pp. 26–29.
[22] Jung, *Man and His Symbols*, pp. 90 ff.
[23] Ibid., p. 153.
[24] Jung, *Alchemical Studies*, p. 337.

and white are alchemical colours, red signifying the sun and white the moon.[25]

The tree also combines development of the spiritual and corporeal as a transformation process:

> In so far as the tree symbolizes the opus and transformation process "tam ethice quam physice" (both morally and physically), it also signifies the life process in general.[26]

Treebeard serves as the guide and agent of psychic and physical growth for two hobbits, Merry and Pippin, who would otherwise have gained nothing from their adventure but calloused feet. Their own growth needs are quite different from those of their older and steadier companion Frodo. They are intellectually less mature (if more lighthearted) and at most times only barely grasp the gravity of the task before them or the extent of the dangers at every turn. Pippin is still an adolescent in years, not entirely responsible and incapable of reading a map. He is a constant trial to Gandalf's patience, and of all the Fellowship the most easily fatigued. Merry is somewhat steadier, but they both speak and behave more like public school pranksters (though without a hint of the Flashman) than companions on a heroic, hopeless quest.

Treebeard's contribution is to the body and soul. His tree-like form is suggestive in itself, but the magical ent-draughts give away Fangorn's secret weapon:

[25] Ibid., p. 339. Note the resemblance of this conceit to the origin of sun and moon as the silver and gold fruit of Laurelin and Telperion, the sacred trees of Valinor described earlier.
[26] Ibid., p. 338.

> The drink was like water, indeed very like the taste of the draughts they had drunk from the Entwash near the borders of the forest, and yet there was some scent or savour in it which they could not describe: it was faint, but it reminded them of the smell of a distant wood borne from afar by a cool breeze at night. The effect of the draught began at the toes, and rose steadily through every limb, bringing refreshment and vigour as it coursed upwards, right to the tips of the hair. Indeed the hobbits felt that the hair on their heads was actually standing up, waving and curling and growing.[27]

Merry and Pippin are tapping the inner reserves of strength, the very growing power of the earth. The effect is quite startling. Gimli the Dwarf remarks only a few days later: "Why, your hair is twice as thick and curly as when we parted; and I would swear that you have both grown somewhat, if that is possible for hobbits of your age."[28] Not even a Halfling may drink the elixir of the ents and emerge from the experience unchanged.

The ent-draughts are more food for the body (or, more precisely in this case, for the biological underpinnings of the psyche) than for the conscious contents of the soul. "Treebeard's draughts may be nourishing," complains Merry, "but one feels the need of something solid. And even *lembas* is none the worse for a change."[29] *Lembas* is the waybread of the Elves and, like the Holy Wafer, the "food for the soul." Merry and Pippin are well nourished. Their roots are securely planted; now it is time for the branches to spread, a resolution we will consider in the next chapter.

[27] Tolkien, *The Lord of the Rings*, II: 64.
[28] Ibid., II: 146.
[29] Ibid.

VIII

númenor regained:

the individuation of the west

EUCATASTROPHE is the term Tolkien used to denote the joyful resolution of the fairy tale,[1] and now we have come to the eucatastrophic moment foreseen from the beginning. It is the time of union, the time of differentiation; the time of sacrifice and renewal, redemption and resolution. The final integration of the theme occurs simultaneously at micro- and macrocosmic levels. It is at once the final act of salvation of the West and the bitter-sweet *beau geste* of its redeemer.

The one-sidedness of the entire society has been a major force from the outset. The spiritual impoverishment of Western Man is the beginning of decline, despite his material and conscious gains:

> No culture is ever complete that swings towards a one-sided orientation. i.e., when at one time the cultural ideal is extraverted, the chief value being given to the *object* and

[1] Tolkien, "On Fairy-Stories" in *Tree and Leaf*, p. 68.

the objective relation, while at the other the ideal is in-
troverted when the supreme importance lies with the individual or *subject* and his relation to the idea.[2]*

The objectivity of Gondor has led to its imbalance, symbolized by its retarded growth (the death of the White Tree) and
the loss of its bridge from past to present, consciousness and
the shadowed unconscious substrate (the failure of the line of
Kings of Númenor, destruction of Osgiliath). Healing can
only come when the abyss is spanned, when the Self emerges
to collect these disparate parts of the psyche and, in the darkness of the unconscious, bind them.

Many forces and beings are involved in the periphery of this
great collective psyche at war with itself, but the pivotal
drama is centered as always around Frodo Baggins, the unwilling Ringbearer. The Ring has always been identified
with the Self; it combines opposites in its form, composition,
and creation:

— It is a symbol of wholeness, symmetrical and perfectly
balanced.
— It is wrought of the purest gold, the alchemical symbol
of the *coincidentia oppositorum*.
— It was formed by the forces of good and evil.†
— Its transcendental teleology is engraved in fiery letters

[2] Jung, *Psychological Types*, p. 95.
* This line of reasoning is indicative of Jung's early embracement of phenomenology, which he admits deriving largely from Kant's *Critique of Pure
Reason*.
† To the extent that the Elven smiths of Eregion contributed their skill and
knowledge unwillingly to the making of the Master Ring. Remember that the
key of Jung's "spectre of the Brocken" existed only because the light of the
conscious cast its shadow upon the mist.

inside and out: "One Ring to rule them all, One Ring to find them/One Ring to bring them all and in the darkness bind them."

The real fate of the Ring is contained in these lines, plus the third, "In the Land of Mordor where the Shadows lie," a verse "long known in Elven-lore," but not entirely understood by the Elves, nor even by Sauron, the author of the chilling incantation. The words of such spells have an irritating habit of coming to pass in undesigned ways, their real message enshrouded in the divine word-salad of the gods. The Delphic Oracle once allowed in the voice of Apollo that a great kingdom would fall, sending the suppliant off on a course of conquest that concluded with the fall of his own kingdom, and fulfilling the promise of the Far Darter in an unpleasant fashion. Similarly, Boromir's dream might be interpreted in more than one way. Boromir notes the prophecy that "Doom is near at hand," and despairs: "Is then the doom of Minas Tirith come at last? But why then should we seek a broken sword?" Aragorn replies that "The words were not *the doom of Minas Tirith.*"[3] *Doom* means fate, that which is set or ordained. Certainly some sort of doom is near at hand, for good or ill.

The ostensible meaning of the lines engraved on the Ring is that all subsidiary rings, the Nine, the Seven, and especially the Three, will ultimately come under the sway of the Ruling Ring. But more than Elven-Rings are converging on Mordor in these last moments of the Third Age, and the doom of the Ringbearer and those who anxiously await the outcome of his quest will be played out "in the Land of Mordor where the Shadows lie."

*

[3] Tolkien, *The Lord of the Rings*, I: 236–37.

Each of the heroes carries a magic talisman, the outward symbols of power. Gandalf's staff is a symbol of maleness, the mystical phallus, which invests him with creative power — the balance of the feminine deity of whom he is only an emissary, the White Lady. Aragorn's sword, once the shards symbolic of the West's division and spiritual impotence, is reforged and invested with the powers of old. But those who must face the Dark Lord in his own land carry gifts that are extensions of their own special personalities, and carry with them the hint of each's fate.

Frodo's is the phial of light given him by Galadriel. The vessel or container is associated with the female aspects of the psyche,[4] and reveals the transcending and guiding nature of the Lady of the Forest. She is the exiled princess of the Noldor who rebelled against the will of the Valar in the Elder Days and came to Middle-earth to regain the silmarils; but she is at the same time the fated agent of Elbereth. Her vision is long: in the mirror of Galadriel she reveals past and future, peers into the unconscious with her all-seeing eyes. The vessel that holds the flickering light is feminine, but the light itself is a symbol of consciousness (*albedo* in the alchemical lexicon that Jung was fond of using). Frodo carries the precious thing for weary miles before it is needed in the darkness of the spider's lair.

Sam's gift is also a container, but within it is the blessing of growth, not the one-sided light of the conscious. The enchanted powder contains the essence of fruitfulness that lies figuratively in the womb of the eternal-feminine, and the seed that will become the last *mallorn* tree east of the sundering seas. It will be the blossoming symbol of the Shire's rebirth, both spiritual and physical, in its growth, its link with the Faërie past and its promise for the future. Sam is

[4] Franz, *C. G. Jung: His Myth in Our Time*, p. 145.

tied to the earth, has both feet planted firmly on the soil of
the Shire; yet he is capable of marshaling the forces of his
own unconscious, where there be dragons. His own individuation is never in doubt, and his fate will ultimately be
far happier than the fates of the high and noble.

Frodo's journey has been an ordeal. His every movement
has been shadowed, literally and figuratively, by
Sméagol/Gollum. This strange personality is now insepara-
ble from Frodo, whom he calls "Master"; and the binding
force of the Ring, hated and desired by both, draws them
nearer. Frodo sinks deeper and deeper into despair and malaise as the Mountains of Ash draw nearer. By the end of the
journey he has lapsed into virtual neurasthenia, and is
dragged on by no more than the dogged determination and
tearful ministrations of Sam. His fate and Gollum's are now
only aspects of the Ring's own malevolent will.

Jung has pointed out that the shadow prefers not to meet
the ego in open combat, particularly on the field of consciousness. The process of individuation suggests the conscious personification of the anima, standing in for the
shadow (and for the unconscious in general), as it "stands
behind" and manipulates the shadow in the unconscious.[5]
The importance of this archetype in the general dynamic of
the psyche is central to this process; it is ". . . a personification of the unconscious in general, and . . . a bridge to the
conscious . . ."[6] Without the confrontation with the anima,
the ego cannot learn to discriminate between anima and
shadow and allow the emergence of the Self as agent of equilibrium.

Gollum, the personification of the unwholesome aspects of
Frodo's own shadow, is not to be confronted at this point.

---

[5] Jung, *Mysterium Coniunctionis*, p. 452.
[6] Jung, *Alchemical Studies*, p. 42.

Shelob, the terrifying and malignant female horror who lurks in the dark places of the earth, is chosen to engage and subdue Frodo. She is not fair to look upon, and manipulates Gollum as Her worshipful servant and grocer, just as the anima stands behind the shadow and pulls the strings. Her power is immense; She has been repressed for millennia in the psyche of Middle-earth, sealed in the caverns of Cirith Gorgor since the ruin of Morgoth in the Elder Days. She nurses her bitter and inarticulate grievances in black silence, spinning Her webs of numen and feeding on the unwary; for She is powerfully hungry, inflated with an unholy lust.

Frodo fights her off in the web-choked tunnels; his weapon is the glowing blade of Sting, his shield the phial of Galadriel, the beacon of consciousness. The sting and light of ego-consciousness are set against the suffocating gloom (negredo) and the arachnid sting of the darkness; and She is fought off. But this is only the ancient ruse of the anima, and She pounces once again from the dark ambush; and though she puts Frodo out of commission She is clearly depotentiated by Sam's blade, thrust through her foul hide by the very weight of her bloated body.*

I have mimicked Tolkien's style here describing the depotentiation of Shelob because it is uncharacteristically lurid on the subject. Shelob is the only negative female figure to be found in any of the stories (I will give Lobelia Sackville-Baggins the benefit of the doubt as an anima symbol; next to Shelob she is Emma Bovary), and Tolkien goes far out of his way to portray her as the eternal-feminine's nasty side, the part that lures to ruin rather than perfection. The spiders of Mirkwood in *The Hobbit* are no more companionable than Shelob, but they have traded size and gender for androgynous mobility. That the difference is made more dra-

---

* The knuckles of Freudian readers will begin to whiten at this point.

matic by the ages of repression is clear from the circumstances. The power of the unconscious complexes is not lessened by nonrecognition — quite the reverse.

But Frodo is afforded little time to gloat. Injected with spider venom, stripped and flogged by orcs, slung about like a battered duffel bag, he is in no mood to do anything but plod glumly onward to the fire-mountain, which is conveniently named Mount Doom. Indeed, Doom is near at hand, and the fate of East and West hangs in the balance.

Sam has helped Frodo as far as he can, and, delayed by a scuffle with the pestiferous Gollum, he hastens up the causeway of Orodruin to the opening of the tunnel that leads to the Cracks of Doom. Tolkien describes the scene in this way:

> Sam came to the gaping mouth and peered in. It was dark and hot, and a deep rumbling shook the air. "Frodo! Master!" he called. There was no answer. For a moment he stood, his heart beating with wild fears, and then he plunged in. A shadow followed him.
>
> At first he could see nothing. In his great need he drew out once more the phial of Galadriel, but it was pale and cold in his trembling hand and threw no light into that stifling dark. He was come to the heart of the realm of Sauron and the forges of his ancient might, greatest in Middle-earth; all other powers were subdued.[7]

Here, in the uttermost depths of the primordial unconscious, the pale flickering light of consciousness does not suffice to light the way; the tiny light flickers and almost dies, as in Jung's dream; and, as in that dream, " a shadow followed him."

Unhelped by the dauntless Sam, a battle is joined there at

[7] Tolkien, *The Lord of the Rings*, III: 196.

the edge of the flame, at the brink of the fire-mountain's abyss, while Frodo and Gollum, ego and shadow, strive desperately for possession of the precious Ring. The battle is uncertain: first one then the other has the mastery. The greater realization of Middle-earth, conscious and unconscious, rests on this tiny pivotal struggle, and the world waits. "The Dark Lord was suddenly aware of him, and his Eye piercing all shadows looked across the plain to the door that he had made . . . Then his wrath blazed in consuming flame, but his fear rose like a vast black smoke to choke him."[8] And, at the same moment, Gandalf "lifted his arms and called once more in a clear voice . . . 'Stand, Men of the West! Stand and wait! This is the hour of doom.' "[9]

The inflated drama of this instant underscores the greater and lesser bipolarity and conflict; light and darkness strive, inner and outer. In the end, Gollum clutches the Ring in triumph, Frodo's gnawed-off finger still attached; but he perishes in the act, swallowed by the cleansing flame. The power of Sauron is ended in a fearful gout of fire and with the toppling of the dark tower.

But in the act of saving the West, Frodo has in a sense precluded his own Self-realization. That possibility fell with Gollum into the fire-mountain, along with the daemonic golden mandala. In time, Frodo will feel the loss, the emptiness that is the cessation of growth. His walking-song is not quite the same:

> . . . *A day will come at last when I*
> *Shall take the hidden paths that run*
> *West of the Moon, East of the Sun.*[10]

---

[8] Tolkien, *The Lord of the Rings*, III: 197.
[9] Ibid., III: 200.
[10] Ibid., III: 272.

And who would know these paths better than he who trod them once before? The metaphorical reference "West of the Moon, East of the Sun" refers to two concepts at once: *centrality* in the sense of movement to the midpoint, and *balance* and *compensation* by the opposition of symbols (albedo + negredo, conscious + unconscious). This is a pretty unambiguous reference to the Self. Its simplicity and power as a symbolic structure influenced the nature of the graphic approach I introduced in Chapter II.

The shadow is just as much a part of us as the ego, and the repudiation of either can only lead to deeper one-sidedness. Frodo instinctively knows this: the salvation of the West has been at the cost of his own personal redemption. His ultimate destination is in the Undying Lands, in the final relinquishing of the joys and sorrows of Middle-earth. He is in good company; Beren and Lúthien before him, and Eärendil, passed to the West when their task was complete. But in seeking the Havens at the end, Frodo is resigning himself to the terrible incompleteness of the psyche. Sam is heartbroken; his best efforts, his finest hours, were spent in his master's service. "I thought," he says tearfully, "you were going to enjoy the Shire too, for years and years, after all you have done." And Frodo replies: "So I thought too, once. But I have been too deeply hurt, Sam. I tried to save the Shire, and it has been saved, but not for me. It must often be so, Sam, when things are in danger: someone has to give them up, lose them, so that others may keep them."[11] The cycle of the savior archetype is complete.

That Frodo's journey is the journey of death is also quite starkly clear. The sound of the sea is the second of Prometheus' gifts, the power to foresee death. The love of Middle-earth, the bond to this world, is strong; but the call of the

[11] Ibid., III: 273.

sea-bell is not to be denied. The sense of foreboding is powerfully described in Poem 15 of *The Adventures of Tom Bombadil:* "The Sea-Bell." This is the poem labeled "Frodos
Dreme" (which came very near being the title of this book),
and ". . . was associated with the dark and despairing
dreams which visited [Frodo] . . . during his last three years
[after the destruction of the Ring]."[12]

The journey over the sea to a land of eternal life as a representation of Man's last journey is as old as Man's concept of
an end of life. The ancient Irish land of the dead, Tir na
nOg, was so depicted, as is the realm of Fisher King in
Chrétien's tale of Perceval, the legends by Hy Breasil, and
the tale of Oisin and Niamh. Procopius identified the Land
of the Blest with Britain ($\beta\rho\iota\tau\tau\iota\alpha$),[13] a notion that may have
pleased and amused Tolkien.

The towers of the Far Downs, from which one may
glimpse the sea, stand on the western marches of the Shire.
They are an object of unease to the hobbits, disquieting
reminders of mortality: "Fear of the sea was the prevailing
mood in the Shire at the end of the Third Age . . ." But
"the thought of the sea was ever-present in the background of
the hobbit imagination."[14] The white towers of Westmarch
are reminiscent of the Dolorous Tower of myth. Brown informs his readers in *Origin of the Grail Legend* that "The oldest
known reference to the tower of the dead is in Pindar: . . .
[The dead] pass by the highway of Zeus to the tower of
Chronus [on the way to the blessed Isles]."[15]

Frodo's friends fare better. Merry and Pippin leave the Shire
on 26 September 3018 as mere shavetails, and return as real
heroes after their fashion, "lordly folk." They have been

---

[12] Tolkien, *The Adventures of Tom Bombadil*, p. 81.
[13] Brown, *The Origin of the Grail Legend*, p. 340.
[14] Tolkien, *The Adventures of Tom Bombadil*, p. 81.
[15] Brown, *The Origin of the Grail Legend*, pp. 355–56.

nourished on *lembas* and strengthened by the life-giving Ent-draughts; and Pippin has even seen the Dark Lord in a seeing-stone. Pippin is (to an extent) a reformed hobbit, a soldier of the Guard of Minas Tirith and the warleader of the Shire. He has, like his friend Merry, secured at least the prize of maturity.

Gandalf and all those whose ties are with the Blessed Realm must now relinquish Middle-earth. Those who wore the Three Rings — Gandalf, Elrond, and Galadriel — must do so, for their powers to heal have vanished into the Cracks of Doom with the rest of the Third Age; in the Fourth Age they are anachronisms. They are incomplete now; the part of them that was rooted in Middle-earth is severed. Like Frodo, they are now one-sided; irredeemably so, for the darker part, which gave them balance, is gone. But in this way, the plan of The One is fulfilled. Man has for better or worse inherited the earth.

But around the drama of these relatively few personalities has swirled the greater, turbulent, individuation of a culture, the rebirth of Middle-earth. The one-sidedness and blind materialism that once gripped Gondor have been replaced by the symbolic reunion of the opposing and compensating conscious and unconscious elements — and unlike Frodo, its savior, the West has reintegrated without losing its foothold in either realm. In the fall of Barad-Dûr and its Dark Lord the shadow has not been banished; the wholesome aspects of the unconscious remain, and they may now be realized in the return of the King and the reforging of Gondor's link with its numinous past. The nature of Aragorn as the uniter of opposites is clearly symbolized in a variety of ways: in the reforging of the sword that was broken, the symbol before of the impotence in the failing line of Kings, and the return of the potency of old with its reformation; in his ability to move in both worlds, walking with equal grace among Men and Elves and speaking their tongues; in his role as warlord of the armies of living and dead, the Men of the West and the wraiths of Dunharrow, spirits which he leads from the dark caves of the mountains into the sunlight to the dismay of his enemies.

Aragorn is fated to undergo his own trial in the Paths of the Dead. These spirits are a dark piece of unfinished business in Gondor's past, the reminder of a broken promise. Order and balance cannot be said to be restored until the wraiths of Dunharrow fulfill their oath of centuries past and find repose. This is Aragorn's duty, and a preordained part of his mission in Middle-earth. The symbol of the King is associated in alchemy in many instances with emergence or some other relationship with the world of darkness. The instrument that Aragorn uses to rally this grisly muster at the Stone of Erech [16] is the replica of the Banner of Elendil, fashioned by Arwen, which depicts in shining embroidery the heirlooms of Númenor:

> *Tall ships and tall kings,*
> > *Three times three.*
> *What brought they from the foundered land*
> > *Over the flowing sea?*
> *Seven stars and seven stones*
> > *And one white tree.* [17]

The references are to stars that formed part of the King's standard, but I find no mention of their heraldic origin; only that they were of shining gems. The conceptual likeness of stars to crystal gems has been discussed earlier, as well as the relationship of both to symbolic representations of the Self.

[16] See the reference to Erech (Uruk) as the point of departure of the Sumerian goddess Inanna (Ishtar) in her seven-stage journey to the underworld, in Henderson and Oakes, *The Wisdom of the Serpent*, p. 101.

[17] Tolkien, *The Lord of the Rings*, II: 179.

The reference to the seven stones (*palantíri*) presumably holds a similar meaning. The number seven is one short of eight, a quaternal number. Like three, it denotes polarity in the alchemist's symbolic repertoire, as well as power, union, and masculine principle.[18] In the days of the Christian Church's early formation, Origen postulated a god-creator separate from what the Gnostics would call The One, plus the "seven Archons" or angels — Michael, Raphael, Gabriel, Suriel, etc. Yahweh is here "the accursed god . . . prince and father of the seven Archons."[19] He completes the quaternion.

The number seven has, moreover, a peculiar and specific meaning in myths of renewal such as the one being played out by Aragorn Elessar:

> Seven is the number most commonly associated with initiation, the number seeming to denote the steps or stages of an inner, as opposed to an outer, journey . . . [The number seven is significant] because of its many connections with initiation . . . associated with ascent leading to the idea of God.[20]

The symbolic meaning of this sort of initiation is a disengagement or withdrawal within one's self. This is explicitly what Aragorn has done, leaving the victorious Rohirrim in dismay and puzzlement, to seek the Paths of the Dead. In the course of the journey Aragorn is himself transformed; the reader leaves him at the Stone of Erech (his Self-emergence symbolized by the magical spherical stone itself), and when he appears again he is the King returned, the war leader whose mere presence turns the tide of battle on the Field of Pelennor. His sword reforged is traced with the once and future role of the King and his own path to that fate: a

[18] Jung, *The Archetypes and the Collective Unconscious*, pp. 233–34.
[19] Jung, *Mysterium Coniunctionis*, p. 402.
[20] Henderson and Oakes, *The Wisdom of the Serpent*, p. 71.

rayed sun and crescent moon bound by seven stars. And his banner records the initiation ordeal (the number seven) into the depths of the personal and collective unconscious psyche, the creative union of opposites (the King of Light and the shadow-men), the fact of the Self (Stone of Erech), and the promise of growth (white tree).

At his accession the wizard Gandalf, always the undaunted hermeneut, reveals a fresh sapling of the white tree to Aragorn, and once again from the roots of the past rise the graceful branches of the human soul that reach ever for the stars.

The crown of Elendil is placed with reverence upon the brow of Aragorn, and the union of opposites is again revealed: for the crown is set with adamant, the stone of unexcelled brilliance and hardness that is associated with the *lapis* of alchemy, and hence with the Self. And his coronation name is Elessar, the Elf-stone.

The Elf-stone, as we have been told in *The Fellowship of the Ring*, is a green gem, identified as beryl; Glorfindel leaves it as a sign to Aragorn that a critical bridge is safe to cross (what but a symbol of the Self would certify the bridge as open to passage and commerce?), and Aragorn's brooch is set with this mineral. The significance of crystals in psychic image has been addressed often. The green stone, however, possesses special importance. Emma Jung describes this aspect of the crystal in *The Grail Legend*:

> The green colour seems to be significant . . . as the colour of vegetation and, in a wider sense, of life, green is obviously in harmony with the Grail [as the object of the psyche's quest] . . . In ecclesiastical symbolism green is the colour of the Holy Ghost or the *anima mundi*, and in the language of the mystics it is the colour of divinity.
>
> In alchemy the emerald also plays an important part . . . The emerald was considered to be the stone of

Hermes . . . This description closely related the emerald to the incorruptible gold. To precious stones it is what gold is to metals, an everlasting, incorruptible substance, the goal of the *opus*. In this context the green colour actually achieves the meaning of life itself. In the alchemical texts the *benedicta viriditas* (the blessed green) also serves as a sign of the reanimation of the material.[21]

Aragorn's coronation name is thus connected symbolically with the following ideas:

— The Self (crystal, lapis)
— The *coincidentia oppositorum* (alchemical signifcance as the counterpart of gold)
— Growth (green color)
— Renewal (green color)
— Hermeneutic (guiding) role (association with Hermes)

The return of the King as the renewer of life is the necessary condition for the rebirth of the White Tree.

We have seen that the greatest historical reversals of Middle-earth have always been accompanied by the romance of human hero and Elf-maiden, and in the return of the King there is a repetition of this theme. Aragorn weds Arwen Undómiel, the daughter of Elrond, thus physically and spiritually reuniting the two kindreds, the sundered lines of Elros and Elrond; and though she sacrifices immortality and her link with the Blessed Realm, he introjects her power for the strengthening of the realm and power of Man. His reign begins on May Day, the day of rebirth; and his marriage is at Midsummer's Day — the Self emerges at the midpoint of the year. The sacred marriage is enacted, the *hieros gamos*.

[21] Jung and Franz, *The Grail Legend*, pp. 164–66.

This set of circumstances is strongly reminiscent of rituals of renewal as old as human society — and as contemporary as the elaborate structures of delusion characteristic of paranoid schizophrenics, since the ideas spring from the same collective unconscious. In *Roots of Renewal in Myth and Madness* the analytical psychologist John Weir Perry has noted the recurrence of certain forms of the renewal theme in ancient myth and clinical experience. The most prevalent are:

1. Establishing the world center as locus
2. Undergoing death
3. Return to the beginnings of time and creation
4. Cosmic conflict as a clash of opposites
6. Apotheosis as king or messianic hero
7. Sacred marriage as a union of opposites
8. New Birth as a reconciliation of opposites
9. New society of the prophetic vision
10. Quadrated world forms[22]

Perry draws examples from the tradition and ritual of Egypt (the Osiris-Horus cycle of ritual rebirth), Mesopotamia (New Year festival of Marduk), and Israel (New Year festival of Yahweh). Had *The Lord of the Rings* dated from an earlier age, the renewal of Middle-earth might have earned a place beside these examples.

The act of renewal is frequently associated with the world center. In the case of Hebrew ritual, "the locus of the rite . . . represents Yahweh's enthronement on his Holy Mount of Zion, whose zenith is the sky and whose nadir is the abyss of the cosmic waters. This sacred mountain therefore establishes a cosmic axis and world center."[23] The most pow-

---

[22] Perry, *Roots of Renewal in Myth and Madness*, p. 82.
[23] Ibid., p. 89.

erful agent of renewal is Gandalf. His symbolic rebirth is enacted on (and under) his own Zion, the great mountain of the Silvertine, in the battle with the terrible demon of shadow and fire; from abysmal waters cold "as the tide of death" to "a narrow space, a dizzy eyrie above the mists of the world."[24] A glance at the map will disclose the Silvertine occupying the geographic center of the known world, a vantage from which Gandalf could hear "the gathered rumour of all lands: the springing and the dying, the song and the weeping, and the slow everlasting groan of overburdened stone."[25]

The ordeal of death is likewise a major aspect of Gandalf's renewal. Osiris is dismembered and drowned by Set in the flood of the Nile. This passion is not spared the Grey Pilgrim: "Then darkness took me, and I strayed out of thought and time, and I wandered far on roads that I will not tell."[26]

The third aspect of the ritual, the return to the beginnings of time and the creation, is implicit in the quote above and in other comments: "There I lay staring upward, while the stars wheeled over, and each day was as long as a life-age of the earth." And, in Caras Galadon, "I tarried . . . in the ageless time of that land where days bring healing not decay. Healing I found, and I was clothed in white."[27]

The theme of cosmic conflict as a clash of opposites is one of the most pervasive in myth. The ritual combat of the avenging Horus against the treachery of Set is symbolic of the struggle of life and death, light and darkness; similarly, the mortal combat between the redeemer Gandalf and the

---

[24] Tolkien, *The Lord of the Rings*, II: 91–92.
[25] Ibid., II: 92.
[26] Ibid.
[27] Ibid.

malevolent Balrog represents the greater clash of opposites that seals the fate of Middle-earth, and the personal denouement of Aragorn and Sauron, of Frodo and Sméagol.

The battle is not easily won. In Perry's words: "For a while death and the enemy hold the upper hand, and there is a period of chaos in which there is a suspension of the normal order of the realm."[28] This is the tone of much of *Lord of the Rings*. The final victory is snatched from the gaping jaws of certain disaster. Indeed, the prelude to the final climactic struggle is the disorder, division, and despair of the West, the failing of the line of the Kings, the humiliation, disintegration, and destruction of Anor, and the threatening twilight of Westernesse. The triumph is all the more glorious, and at once harder and more bitter, for the long years of defeat.

The apotheosis of Gandalf is made most explicit in *The Two Towers*. His transformation — the change of character, the kindling of the inner light of Valinor, raiment of the Holy Ones, has been discussed in an earlier chapter. Similarly Aragorn, after his own journey on the Paths of the Dead and the final battle before the Iron Gates of Mordor, is subtly transformed; Sam scarcely recognizes the rascally Strider arrayed as a king and crowned with the winged helmet of Elendil. Finally, the Ringbearer himself, the tiny pivotal figure whose sacrifice brings about the defeat of the Enemy, is never the same hobbit. Middle-earth is no longer for him, and his place is among the passengers on the last ship.

The new society of the prophetic vision is both optimistic and bitter. The future is Man's, for better or worse, the old ways (as Saruman glimpsed) are gone. Soon there will be no

[28] Perry, *Roots of Renewal in Myth and Madness*, p. 84.

trace of the Firstborn, the People of the Stars, but the memory of their glory and their tears. Yet Man's hope is founded upon the power of Númenor, remembrance of things past and a pledge of things to come. Past and future are made one in the ritual coronation and the sacred marriage, the opposites united. Yet there is the disquieting knowledge that the Dark Lord is not forever vanquished, since he dwells not in time or space, but within the psyche. Always, "after a defeat and a respite," he will return and the cycle of redemption and renewal will be repeated, just as Osiris dies and is reborn with the flooding of the Nile, as the grain is sown and gathered.

The quaternal form of the world is stated in terms of time rather than geography. The chronology of Middle-earth must be altered. The Third Age has ended, the Fourth Age now begins. The Fourth Age completes the quaternion, the long awaited fourth part of the eternal pattern. Jung writes:

> The quaternity is an archetype of almost universal occurrence. It forms the logical basis for any whole judgement.
> . . . Three is not a natural coefficient of order, but an artificial one. There are always four elements, four prime qualities, four colors, four castes, four ways of spiritual development, etc. So, too, there are four aspects of the psychological orientation . . .[29]

And Aniela Jaffé clarifies:

> A quaternity or quaternion often has a 3 + 1 structure, in that one of the terms composing it occupies an exceptional

[29] Jung, *Psychology and Religion: West and East*, p. 167.

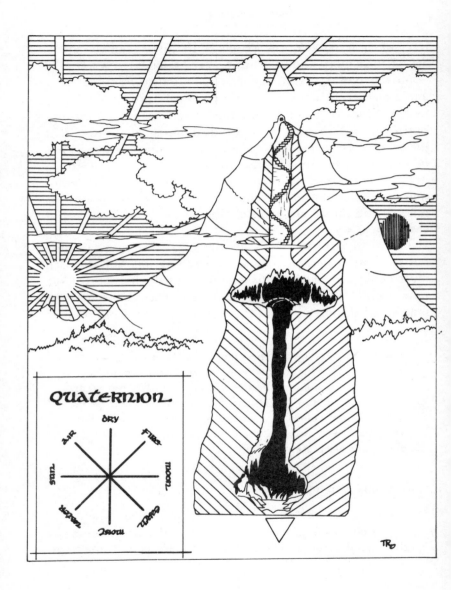

> position or has a nature unlike the others . . . This is the
> "Fourth," which, added to the other three, makes them
> "One," symbolizing totality.[30]

The quaternion also applies to multiples of four (as in Figure 12) or in the "eightfold path" (q.v.). The One Ring completes the quaternion of the One and the Three, the Elven-Rings; and the One and the Seven, those of the Dwarves. Men are the exception. The number three, as we have seen, is a "disturbed" number, one short of quaternity and balance. This is very much a characteristic of Man and not of the Elves.

This 3 + 1 characteristic cited by Jaffé also helps us to understand the loss of the Elven-Rings' power to heal after the destruction of the Master Ring. The Three are named the rings of air (on Elrond's finger), water (the feminine symbol of the womb and hence possessed by Galadriel), and fire (worn by Mithrandir as renewer of strength). The Master Ring completes the four elements, by virtue of its forging in the fiery cracks of the earth, and together they represent the essence of creation: earth, air, fire, water. We might say that

[30] Jaffé, editorial note in *Memories, Dreams, Reflections*, p. 416.

FIGURE 12. SILVERTINE

As the prelude to apotheosis, Gandalf must undergo his own transformation in the battle with the Balrog. This drawing of the scene of the conflict underscores this event's commonality with other myths of renewal. Silvertine is seen as the center of the world, the axis of creation, from the depths of the earth to the pinnacle that touches the heavens. The first blows are struck at the border, on the literal and figurative bridge between light and dark, and the fight rages down into the depths and up again into the realm of the sun. The nature of the battlefield and its place in the greater topography of the world is set against the alchemists' quaternion, adapted here from Jung's sketch in *Mysterium Coniunctionis*, p. 247.

there is a sort of power in this completeness that is greater than the sum of its parts, a synergic force that captures the power of creation by recapitulating its elements. The ring of earth is the uniter: perfect, symmetrical, and forged of purest gold, the *coincidentia oppositorum*. Despite its evil essence (necessary as an element of the world since evil in the form of Melkor's song was present from the first) the Master Ring is the necessary foundation of the magical pattern. Without it the pattern is in disarray, disturbed and impotent; and without that connecting link the Eldar are "not of this world" in the literal sense, and must seek the Havens. This is the same theme that directs Frodo's fate and Gandalf's: with the loss of completeness they must renounce the world they saved for others.

Indeed, the cycle foreseen in *The Silmarillion* is now complete, and in its completeness is recapitulated the development of the human psyche:

In the First Age, Man is primitive, his consciousness is awkward and tied to (and dominated by) the unconscious. It is the age of Elves, the time of the realm of Faërie.

In the Second Age, with the fall of Morgoth, Man believes

FIGURE 13. EUCATASTROPHE: THE WHITE TREE

The resolution of Middle-earth's dilemma is summarized in this drawing. The White Tree, saved from the wreck of Númenor by the Elf-friends, has regained life through the efforts of Elendil's heir Elessar (Aragorn), whose initiation and transformation are symbolized by the seven stars and seven stones, and the rayed sun, symbol of masculinity and of Man's fate. The opposites are united finally with the sacred marriage to Arwen (*hieros gamos*), in which the sundered lines of Eärendil's sons are reforged; her symbol is the crescent moon, a feminine image and the planetary body associated with the Eldar. The instrument of individuation is the central mandala design built of the Ring and the *coincidentia oppositorum* as a quaternion, inscribed with the Doom of the Ring: *One Ring to rule them all, One Ring to Find them/One Ring to bring them all and in the darkness bind them.*

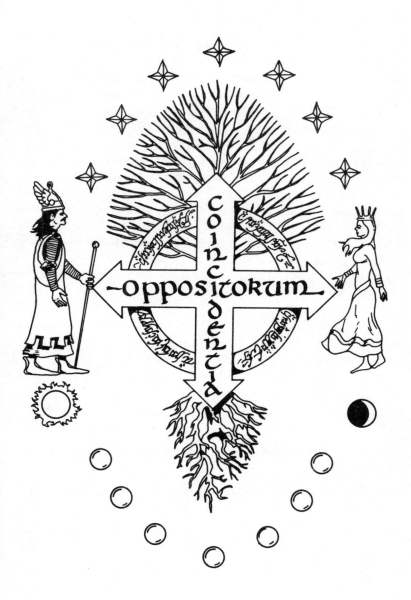

he has come of age; his consciousness expands from the magnificent island-empire of Númenor. But in that expansion the contact with the past and the archetypal substrate is lost; Númenor vanishes beneath the waves of the unconscious.

In the Third Age the conscious and unconscious are estranged; the unity with nature and magic is sold for material gain, and neurosis results from the spiritual impoverishment of the West. In the end, the West is guided through the trials of individuation to the realization of the Self.

The Fourth Age is the age of balance, the once and future golden age in which the psyche of Man is in equilibrium; the final goal, the last unfolding of Man's potential, is now possible, and the last strain of the Song of the Holy Ones.

And now the song is complete.

ix

archetype and allegory

THE POINT of this book has not been that *The Lord of the Rings* is about Self-realization. Obviously, it is about a heroic quest undertaken by those who would be least expected to exhibit heroism. It would be unfair (and, I think, inaccurate) to suggest that Professor Tolkien was trying to teach us a lesson about theory and construct in analytical psychology, nor yet to present an allegory, a sort of psychological *Pilgrim's Progress*.

The author's dislike of allegory, "in all its manifestations," is well known to his many admirers. He insists explicitly in the preface to the American edition that the work was not intended to contain any such message or contemporary or historical reference, and disavowed any intended analogy between the present political climate and the conflict between East and West which dominates the story of Middle-earth. The reader may fairly ask why, in the face of this denial of any underlying message, I would have the rudeness to suggest just the opposite. The answer is, of course, that I am not suggesting any such thing; and I believe that the subcreator of Middle-earth would absolve me of any such hubris were he alive at this writing.

Tolkien stated in almost the same breath as his repudiation of allegory that "many confuse 'applicability' with 'allegory'; but the one resides in the freedom of the reader, and the other in the purposed domination of the author."[1] Certainly no message, as such, is intended to dominate either story or reader — at least not by the author's contrivance — nor is there a direct applicability to the affairs of Men and nations. The themes are somewhat more delicate than that would suggest, yet we have at least glimpsed their ancient power in these few pages (if not in the original works, quite without critical commentary).

In his treatise "On Fairy-Stories," Tolkien has a few choice words for those who would dissect a myth "to see what it is made of":

> There are many elements in fairy-stories . . . that can be studied without tackling the main question [of where they came from]. Such studies are, however, scientific (at least in intent); they are the pursuit of folklorists and anthropologists: that is of people using the stories not as they were meant to be used, but as a quarry from which to dig evidence, or information, about matters in which they are interested. A perfectly legitimate procedure in itself — but ignorance or forgetfulness of the nature of the story (as a thing told in its entirety) has often led such inquirers into strange judgements. To investigators of this sort recurring similarities . . . seem especially important . . . misleading in particular if it gets out of their monographs and into books about literature. They are inclined to say that any two stories that are built around the same folklore-motive,

---

[1] Tolkien, *The Lord of the Rings*, I: 8.

or are made up of a generally similar combination of such motives, are "the same stories."[2]

However, I refuse to interpret this as a curse on my present project. This gently admonitory passage is really saying two things: the whole of a story is greater than the sum of its parts, and (in effect) psychiatrists who go to striptease shows to watch the people watch the girls are (1) not learning much that is useful, and (2) missing the real action. I exclude myself from both categories. I am not talking about a similarity in the stories and myths themselves, but rather a broad commonality of repetitive folklore-motives, those to which he refers in his comments, and others much more subtle. And this is not saying that they are "the same story"; only that certain moods and devices are the same, and that these tell us something about the creative minds that assembled them. These motives or affect images are, of course, merely the way in which common instincts personify themselves — that is, they are the archetypes which collectively constitute the fountainhead of human expression. I hardly think Professor Tolkien would challenge the notion of fairly constant human motives which appear again and again in myth and folklore, since he had no qualms about using them to fashion a good story.

He suggested three sources for fairy-stories, given the commonality of theme: invention, inheritance, and diffusion. The first suggests that the theme is an innate part of the storyteller, and springs independently, time and again, from these independent sources; and the author adds that "if we believe that sometimes there occurred the independent striking out of similar ideas and themes and devices, we simply

---

[2] Tolkien, "On Fairy-Stories" in *Tree and Leaf*, p. 24.

multiply the ancestral inventor but do not in that way clearly understand his gift."[3] Given the context and the time that the paper was presented, this is probably a reference to Jung; it would be rather imaginative to offer it as anything else. This suggests, at least, that at the time (1939) Tolkien recognized the existence and pertinence of Jungian ideas, but preferred to leave such speculations to Jungians.

A further discussion in Humphrey Carpenter's biography of Tolkien adds that:

> Some have puzzled over the relation of Tolkien's stories and his Christianity, and have found it difficult to understand how a devout Roman Catholic could write with such conviction about a world where God is not worshipped. But there is no mystery. *The Silmarillion* is the work of a profoundly religious man. It does not contradict Christianity but complements it. There is in the legends no worship of God, yet God is indeed there . . . Tolkien cast his mythology in this form because he wanted it to be remote and strange, and yet at the same time *not to be a lie*. He wanted the mythological and legendary stories to express his own moral view of the universe . . . When he wrote *The Silmarillion* Tolkien believed that in one sense he was writing the truth. He did not suppose that precisely such peoples as he described, "elves," "dwarves," and malevolent "orcs," had walked the earth and done the deeds that he recorded. But he did feel, or hope, that his stories were in some sense an embodiment of a profound truth. This is not to say that he was writing an allegory; far from it. Time and again he expressed his distaste for that form of literature. "I dislike allegory wherever I smell it," he once said, and similar phrases echo through his letters to readers of his book. So in what sense did he suppose *The Silmarillion* to be "true"?[4]

[3] Tolkien, "On Fairy-Stories" in *Tree and Leaf*, p. 27.
[4] Carpenter, *J. R. R. Tolkien*, p. 99.

Of this "profound truth," Carpenter suggests the occurrence of " 'a sudden glimpse of the underlying reality or truth.' "

> Certainly while writing *The Silmarillion* Tolkien believed that he was doing more than inventing a story. He wrote of the tales that make up the book: "They arose in my mind as 'given' things, and as they came, separately, so too the links grew. An absorbing, though continually interrupted labour (especially, even apart from the necessities of life, since the mind would wing to the other pole and spread itself on linguistics): yet always I had the sense of recording what was already "there," somewhere: not of "inventing."[5]

This is an enlightening series of thoughts. The point of the book is, of course, that Tolkien *was* recording "what was already 'there' ": the subcreator's stream of consciousness flowing eagerly through the watercourses of primordial affect, and these images emerging into enchanting reality for him and for millions of readers. "The mind would wing to the other pole and spread itself on linguistics." This is a significant enough comment to a Jungian; the contemplation of word origins is a conscious task, while the release of archetypal images is unconscious (and these tasks would be described explicitly as "polar" by an analytical psychologist). Tolkien has clearly made an insightful speculation on the source of his inspiration.

In any case, it would be accurate to say that *The Lord of the Rings* is not an allegory in the strict sense of the word, since the author does not prescribe conclusions for the reader.*

---

[5] Ibid., p. 100.
* It is not impossible, of course, for archetype and allegory to coexist. Bunyan's *Pilgrim's Progress* is overtly allegorical and yet very much in the grip of primordial image.

The reader may or may not be aware of any self-interpretation of the book — the vast majority certainly do not — since it is finally a *story*, written to be enjoyed rather than dissected. The absence of allegory does not preclude the presence of theme. Indeed, without theme there is no story, only gibberish. Nor need that theme be so salient as to overwhelm the reader's enjoyment of the story (as Tolkien's theme certainly does not), since this would seriously erode the theme's impact — nobody would read it. Letting message, even a message subtle, diffuse, and largely unintentional, get in the way of the story is, like the *h* in Thames, "a folly without warrant."

Tolkien's currency is the myth, particularly the North European body of myth. More than one investigator has beaten this subject ferociously into the soil in a misguided attempt to find the elusive "point" to the whole thing. I find this line of inquiry something of a dry hole, even less rewarding than the relentless digging into the obscure origins of words and names; this may be satisfying in its own right, but gives little clue about the nature of the work unless the words and sources are viewed in a greater context of the common motives that produced them.

The northern myths have only an antiquarian fascination for most readers, little of the marvelous potency that once resided in their telling beside the hearth or under the stars. For one thing, sources such as the Eddic sagas sprang from a mentality quite different from the modern one which so readily embraces Middle-earth; Midgard would not be so appealing. The heroes struggle against a grim, contradictory fate, which finally gobbles them up on the day of Ragnarökk. Had the War of the Ring followed that line of imagery, East and West would have fought to the death, resulting in the devastation of the world, the annihilation of the Valar and the minions of Sauron, and the rebirth of Middle-earth under the gentle ministrations of The One. Tolkien's mythology, in short, borrows from the past, from the psychological heritage of Northern Europe; but the telling is a far cry from those sources. The archetypes remain the same, but the conscious guise changes as consciousness changes with cultural context. Old archetypes lose potency unless they can be couched in forms appropriate to the time.

Interestingly, *The Silmarillion* seems to lack this contemporary appeal. Its form and mood are disquietingly archaic, wholly devoid of the mercurial humor of the hobbit stories. The earlier work also lacks the meticulous balance of symbolic structure. It is an oddly amorphous retelling of the trials of the races. In an odd way it is more like methodical history — an attempted retelling of actual, rather than fanciful, events. Despite its fantastic elements, it might just as easily have been an accurate portrayal of the way things actually came to pass in a world where dragons dwelt and dwarves hewed stone. At this writing, *The Silmarillion* has been on the *New York Times* best seller list for many weeks. During that time it has never been listed as an editor's choice. It is not an easy work to wade through, even for a confirmed Elf-friend (a biblical scholar might have an easier time). The charm of Middle-earth is compelling, and perhaps the niceties of packaging are overwhelmed by the fact that a large reading public has been primed, made sensitive by a world created as our own should have been. A friend once admitted mild exasperation upon completion of *The Lord of the Rings* that there was no more. Now there is.

The question remains of Tolkien's intent. It is pointless to suggest that there was none, since all stories have an intent. I have spent some time and effort to point out the recurrence of certain symbolic themes (whatever the original author chooses to call them), and suggest their applicability to the study of human psychology. Tolkien was not a psychologist by disposition, and insisted that his stories are meant to be taken without exhaustive analysis — perhaps he kept in mind Gandalf's admonition about such reductionism — and enjoyed for what they say they are. This leaves a delicate problem.

One alternative is that Tolkien had, through years of exposure, an intuitive feel for the elements of myth and fairy tale that influenced the structure of his work without his conscious intent or knowledge. If we believe a tithe of what Jung said, then we must acknowledge the possibility of this influence. If Tolkien was sensitive to these devices, his stories would be at least a rough echo of the horns of Elfland. In this case, the structured symbolism would be a coincidental reflection of the underlying strains of commonality, originating from the human psyche (or the *Ainulindalë*) and finding expression thus in the story of Middle-earth.

The second alternative is more difficult for most reviewers to accept uncritically, but I would be shortchanging the reader if I did not present it. It is simply the suggestion that Tolkien was *directly* influenced by Jungian theory and consistently wove this structure into his work.

I chose to regard this possibility as a *null hypothesis;* that is, I would seek to *disprove* it (since it is unlikely ever to be proven) rather than taking a strictly expository approach. The latter leads us to see what we *want* to see (a taint I will certainly be accused of anyway). I have encountered no source that was informed on Tolkien's tastes and attitudes that was willing to allow for the possibility of a Jungian influence.* This, however, does not disprove in itself the hy-

---

* Mrs. Anne N. Barrett of Houghton Mifflin Company, Tolkien's biographer Humphrey Carpenter, Dr. Joseph L. Henderson, and Christopher Tolkien expressed doubt. The last did not exclude the possibility of his father's exposure to Jung, but dismissed any suggestion that it may have influenced his mythology.

pothesis. The final evaluation must rest on the principle of parsimony: without certainty, we should not ignore the simplest theory that satisfies the known facts.

In most fairy tales the themes have been distorted by time and cultural influence, and by censorship of the church and of parents, who may, as times become more "enlightened," find the themes too frightening for children (who would probably laugh at such silly notions) as they approach the original sources. These relationships are much more clearly displayed in Tolkien's work, sometimes almost compellingly obvious. One of the chief difficulties in writing this book has been the organization of sudden floods of complex association that were triggered by one line of inquiry after another; as if the history of Middle-earth had been composed as a Jungian primer. It is not entirely certain that the theme of Self-realization that emerges could be accidental; its appearance in every level of the stories is rather compelling, and suggesting alternative hypotheses seems to present a gentle challenge to parsimony.

Yet despite its presence, the theme does not overpower either story or reader — as Tolkien clearly intended that it not. His friend C. S. Lewis was not so delicate, perhaps because of the zealousness of his late embracement of Christianity and chosen role as lay theologian. My fifth-grade daughter had no trouble reconciling *The Lion, the Witch, and the Wardrobe* with the gospels. The Land of Narnia, for all its enchantments, is as unlikely a place even to children as Middle-earth is at least wistfully believable to adults. Tolkien's world is a "real" world, and its parallels are not to be found in comparative culture and physical geography, but in the construct-geography of the mind.

Tolkien's attachment to theological speculation (such as it was, and in the guise of feigned history) is also a matter for consideration, and a point on which he and Jung were probably irreconcilable. Tolkien was a believer. Although Jung admired the Roman Catholic Church for its rich fund of available symbols, beside which the Protestant view of godhead was somewhat undernourished, he was not willing to accept a God in the *objective* sense, and saw no reason to do so. God was to Jung a very real and potent force, but a force within the psyche, not outside it; this approach casts God in the role of an archetype identified with the Self, an instinct that Man *projects* from internal potential to external reality in religious beliefs. This would have been an unappealing concept for Tolkien, as would Jung's preoccupation with religious viewpoints of Gnosticism, with its god that combines good and evil. Tolkien's approach to the problem of evil is very Christian in its personification of evil as the rebellious Melkor and his coterie of fallen angels.

I cannot deny that Tolkien took great pains to debunk any ideas of purposeful influence (although he fell far short of dismissing it entirely). Perhaps he believed that examination of Frodos Dreme through the foreign spectacles of psychology or anthropology might fatally weaken its enchantment, like the communion that is finally reduced to no more than a munch of dry wafer and a sip of wine. I can sympathize with the author on that point, having been required as a victim of Plebe English to write a most unwilling paper on the theme of sacrifice in *Billy Budd*—an experience which, for me at least, forever spoiled a basically good yarn. On the other hand, I do not believe that imposing, at least tentatively, the perspectives of analytical psychology weakens either the tale itself or its impact on me.

Tolkien was intimately familiar with many forms of Man's subcreation, from *Beowulf* to Perrault to the *Red Fairy Book*. It is difficult to imagine that he was unfamiliar with Jung's work, since any deeply educated academic in the fields of literature and comparative folklore would have to be remarkably isolated to avoid such exposure. Tolkien does not mention Jungian ideas; I do not imply that Tolkien was a closet Jungian, merely that there is no evidence of lengthy study in the area. Lengthy study would not have been necessary, nor would the author have been obligated to footnote any such incidental debt — archetypes are, if nothing else, public domain.

But that Tolkien was influenced to any degree by analytical psychology is probably an indefensible assertion. Certainly the books were not written with a copy of *Symbols of Transformation* at hand, and enough appears to be known of the writer's tastes and moral predispositions to reject any wholesale embracement of analytical psychology as a deliberate theme. Before abandoning that alternative altogether, however, I feel obliged to offer two shreds of evidence, which Jungian readers will surely bring to my attention if I neglect them. They are suggestions, at least, that Tolkien might have had at least some firsthand knowledge, which he was willing to allude to in print.

The first concerns the rallying point of memory for Western Man, the lost Númenor. Númenor was the symbol of the original dissociation of the Children of God from the will of the Valar, and incidentally from their ties to their own origin; and also the promise of their reintegration. Its loss, symbolically into the darkness of the unconscious, is the real beginning of Man's movement to one-sidedness, and the powerful affect-image associated with renewal.

The association of Númenor with the Jungian terms numen, numinosum, etc., is very likely. The latter term (which was actually borrowed from Rudolf Otto) derives from the Latin *nuere*, to nod assent; it has a broader meaning of divine assent, divine will, the power of the gods accruing to a person, act, or idea.[6] This implication led Jung to use

---

[6] Derived from *numen*, *-inis*; in the literal sense of a nod, but also in the sense of "an expression of will, *command, consent* . . . esp. of a deity, *the*

the word to describe the energy stored in unconscious complexes. The symbolic stature of Númenor as a powerful emotional relic of Man's past implies that both words derived from the same source for the same reason. This is one of the very rare instances (I know of no other) in which Tolkien draws from a Latin root rather than from his favorites, Welsh, Finnish, and Anglo-Saxon. This would be less puzzling if the term came from Jung (or even Otto) rather than independently from the classical source. The name is taken to mean "Westland" or "Westernesse,"[7] and if the guess concerning its origin is correct, we might be justified in searching for other direct influences.

The second intriguing point concerns Jung's name for the collection of fantasies by which he recorded his personal journey to Self-realization: "A folio volume bound in red leather, contains . . . fantasies couched in elaborately literary form and language, set down in calligraphic Gothic script, in the manner of medieval manuscripts."[8] He embellished these pages with his own illuminated drawings. These illustrations, many of them mandalas not much different from the designs that occupied Tolkien's artistic efforts for a time, were part of what Jung called the Red Book. The parallel with the hobbits' chronicle, the *Red Book of Westmarch*, is rather startling. They are physically identical (handwritten red leather-bound manuscripts), and similar in theme. The one recorded the individuation of a man in subjective speculation, the other the individuation of a people and culture, Tolkien's own Westmarch, to which he bequeathed at the very least a conscious realization of the unexpressed primordial forces.

---

divine will, *divine command*: deo cuius numini parent omnia . . . " This leads to its use as *"the might of a deity, majesty, divinity."* Simpson, *Cassell's New Latin Dictionary*, pp. 398–99.
[7] Tolkien, *The Silmarillion*, p. 414.
[8] Jaffé, editorial note in *Memories, Dreams, Reflections*, p. 213.

Of course, this could be pure coincidence, or — more likely still — a reference to Andrew Lang and the *Red Fairy Book*. The extent of direct influence, if any, will probably never be measured conclusively; but the direct kinship through the universality of mythical themes remains as evidence of archetypes, their existence and their effect on human mentality. Perhaps this is the most powerful lesson, the unguessed source of appeal of Tolkien's work.

This work has not been one of scientific inquiry; there are no empirically verifiable hypotheses, merely speculations and the investigation of patterns of idea and emotion. I began this book with preconceived notions of what I would find, or at least a heightened mental set. This is not an orderly or objective way to approach most subjects, and certainly does not prove or disprove anything; some of my professors would criticize me severely if I suggested anything else. Consequently I cannot merely close by offering a smug "Q.E.D." The conclusions are left up to the reader as his experience and preference lead him.

If any proof of Jung's theories (or, more precisely, supporting evidence, since proof is an elusive goal in psychology) is ever offered, it will probably originate on the frontiers of neurophysiology, as we come to understand what mentality truly is in functional terms. Late research in hemispheric lateralization, the role of ribonucleic acid molecules in memory and cognition, and new studies of the heritability of experience may in time yield a demonstration that archetypes are based on solid neuroanatomical substrata, and we will be able to stop regarding them in uncomfortable metaphysical terms. But that time has not yet come.

Finally, I hope that devoted readers who have lived unashamed the fantasies of Middle-earth will forgive my interpretations. I am not trying to impose a dry theoretical framework on the practice of enchantment, nor to drag the act of subcreation kicking and screaming into the clinical consulting room. Hobbits delight in genealogy, and I have my own academic preferences quite far removed from analytical psychology. Perhaps, after all, there is room for speculation on the writing of good fairy tales, as long as the tales themselves are not damaged in the process (as I believe that Tolkien's work will somehow survive the present critique more or less intact). The secret is, I suppose, in breaking the white light and examining its magnificent spectrum to see what it is made of, then being careful to put it back together. I have tried to do just that. Whether I have succeeded or not is for the reader to conclude.

West Point, New York
August 1978

GLOSSARY OF KEY TERMS
BIBLIOGRAPHY
INDEX

GLOSSARY OF KEY TERMS

AFFECT-IMAGE

A more contemporary name for the archetype; *affect* refers to the emotional domain of behavior, hence the term suggests the self-personification of an emotional complex.

ALCHEMY

A medieval protochemistry that sought the secrets of certain scientific and philosophical problems, e.g., the method of transmuting base metals into gold, the discovery of the universal solvent. Jung pointed out that the alchemists' tests and traditions were unusually rich in the symbolic promptings of the unconscious, and hence worthy of study by psychologists. See Jung, *Collected Works*, 12, 13, 14.

ALBEDO

Light, brightness; a representation of the conscious in men (see discussion of *fanar*, pp. 91, 102). Albedo is an alchemical term referring to white or clear light or color; alternative descriptors include negredo (darkness), rubedo (redness), citrinitas (yellow), and viriditas (green). Significance of certain colors is discussed in the text.

ANALYTICAL PSYCHOLOGY
The accurate title of the school of psychology founded by Jung. The Freudian school is generally referred to as the *psychoanalytic;* Adler's set of theories is usually called *individual psychology.*

ANIMA
The archetype which personifies the collective image of Man's experience of Woman.
The analogue of the anima in women is the *animus.*

ANIMAL
An archetype related to human experience with, and evolution from, animals. As a symbol (in dreams, myth, art, fairy tales, etc.) it may represent instinctual urges or unrestrained libido.

ANXIETY
A "free-floating fear" in the clinical sense, the basic characteristic of neurosis; from the German *Angst.* This term also has immense importance in Freudian theory.

ARCHETYPE
A "primordial image" in Jung's early theory development; an innate predisposition formed by generations of psychic evolution. One modern analytical psychologist prefers the use of "affect-image" (q.v.). Archetypes include God, savior, anima(us), Trickster, Self, quaternity, Wise Old Man, animal, divine child, and others. They find conscious expression through *symbols.* See Chapter II.

BEHAVIOR
The measurable responses of an organism reacting to and operating on its environment.

BEHAVIORISM
One of the major schools of psychology. Behaviorism is an empirical approach, which, in its purest form, seeks to operationalize (make measurable) the behavior of organisms by reducing their activities to discrete responses (R) and antecedent and consequent stimuli (S), which prompt or signal the organism and reinforce or punish its behaviors. For this reason, it is also called R-S psychology.

COINCIDENTIA OPPOSITORUM

The union of opposites; the term, like many of Jung's, is borrowed from alchemy, and represents the archetype of balance and compensation, often associated with the Self. The Taoist principles of yin and yang illustrate a symbolic rendering of this image.

COLLECTIVE UNCONSCIOUS

This is a conceptual foundation stone of analytical psychology. The collective unconscious is composed of those elements of the psyche that are outside the level of conscious awareness and that are shared by all members of the species. The collective unconscious may be regarded as the matrix from which the archetypes may emerge. Common themes in myth, religion, art, and literature emanate from this common phylogenetic psyche.

COMPENSATION

This concept is central to the idea of a differentiated conscious and unconscious structure. Elements in each realm have a balancing or compensating (complementing) element in the other.

COMPLEX

Originally coined by Alfred Adler, this term has a special meaning in the Jungian idiom. A complex is a cluster of thoughts, emotions and predispositions, which cluster together and share energy because of similarity. This energy is called *numen* (q.v.); mental disorder is often heralded or accompanied by intrusion of complexes into consciousness.

CONSCIOUS, CONSCIOUSNESS

Thoughts and feelings that are in the realm of awareness are said to be conscious. The center of the conscious part of the psyche is the ego complex; the outward, collectively inspired, presentation of the conscious ego is the persona (q.v.).

CONSTRUCT

A concept that is conceived ("constructed") in the formulation, statement, and testing of theories. It may not be directly measurable; that is, it may be a thing or process inferred to exist as a common-sense convenience (e.g., gravity, intelligence) or as part of a more complex semantic framework for theoretical models (ego, libido).

DEPOTENTIATION

The release or redirection of built-up libido stored in a complex, usually implying its reallocation for healthier use. The term is applied to the individuation process in which the anima is confronted in a conscious dialectic and its numen depotentiated and made available to the Self for its emergence and transcendence.

DETERMINISM

The philosophical principle that, when applied to behavior, suggests that organisms respond to their environments in ways that have been fixed by instincts or previously acquired patterns of action. The principal philosophical implication of this approach is in the matter of *free will;* if behaviors in the present are predetermined, for instance, by situations and responses learned in the past, there isn't any. Determinism is particularly important to the psychoanalytic and Behaviorist theories.

DRAGON

Any of a variety of mythological beasts, especially those that are theriomorphic combinations of serpent and bird (*drakes*). Among other things a dragon may symbolize the union of opposites, by virtue of its combinatory form (the chthonic or earthy snake, the free soaring bird). See Chapter IV for further discussion.

EGO

The center of the conscious realm of the psyche, also called the ego-complex. This is the cluster of thoughts, habits, emotions, and physical attributes which comprises the personal identity. It is associated with the persona, or public self. The term "ego" is also used in Freudian psychoanalytic theory and, more rarely and in different contexts, in some other psychodynamic and Humanistic theories.

ENTROPY

From the Second Law of Thermodynamics: the tendency of all things to break down to their simplest components, to depotentiate or "run down." This is the opposite of creative synthesis in the psychological sense.

GNOSTICISM

Gnosticism was a proto-Christian religious sect centered in the Middle East in the first centuries of the Christian Era. Jung used certain Gnostic concepts, particularly acceptance of the dual nature of God, in illustrating religion's origins in the structure and dynamics of the psyche.

GOD

Jung adopted more or less Voltaire's position on the subject of a deity: if there were none, we would have to create him. In Jungian theory, the idea of God is a projection or conscious symbol of the Self, personification of balance and perfection.

GOLD

In the alchemistic tradition, Gold represents the *coincidentia oppositorum*, the hoped-for end product of the search for perfection. Gold things often carry this symbolic meaning in human expression.

HERMAPHRODITE

An archetypal image of the union of opposites; the connotation is not at all sexual in the biological sense. A more descriptive term is "psychic androgyny."

HERMES

The Graeco-Roman god whose roles included the conduct of souls to the nether world; hence the symbolic guide. The wizard Radagast is associated by name as well as task to Hermes/Mercury.

HERMENEUTIC

Specifically used by me to denote the role of the analytical psychologist in his interaction with the analysand in guiding him toward Self-realization (fulfilling Hermes' task). I have used this term also to denote archetypal personifications with similar functions.

HERO

This is a personification of the Self as a prodigious human (or animal), often a savior in the more developed stages. The union of opposites may be associated with the Hero (e.g., Christ as God and Man, Word and Flesh) as well as other archetypes. See Trickster as early stage of hero cycle.

HIEROS GAMOS

This is the divine marriage, symbolizing the archetypal union of opposites, often in the context of the ritual of renewal. The ritual of the Year-King in primitive agricultural groups, the divine union of Osiris and Isis in the rebirth *Djed* festival, and the eucatastrophic union of Aragorn and Arwen illustrate this tradition.

HUMANISM

This describes a collection of theories that take a generally mentalistic, optimistic, or nondeterministic view of human nature. The name carries with it (in the psychological context) the implication that humans are not, at the very least, rats. The general title includes phenomenological theories (Rogers, Lewin, Goldstein), which stress the uniqueness of individual human experience; existentialist theories (Binswanger, Boss, Frankl), which are concerned with Man's experience of his place in the universe; and George Kelly's constructive alternativism. It differs collectively from psychodynamic theories and from Behaviorism partly by emphasizing goal-directed (teleological) motives rather than driven, deterministic ones. Analytical psychology can be characterized as bridging the gap between Humanistic and psychodynamic theories, since it meets the criterion of viewing personality as a dynamic interaction of internal forces while maintaining a goal-motivation (Self-realization).

IDENTIFICATION

A mechanism or process, principally in psychodynamic theories, in which one mental force or activity takes on the characteristics of another, or of an outside object or person. In Freudian theory, identification is an ego defense mechanism — most dramatically the method of resolving castration anxiety by identifying with the father and assuming (introjecting) his values and beliefs, the major step in developing the social consciousness that Freud called the superego. In Jungian theory, one element — usually the ego —

may identify with another. In the cases cited in the text, the ego may become inflated (q.v.) by identification with an archetype. See text, Chapter VI.

INDIVIDUATION

This is the psychodynamic process by which the Self is realized; the major therapeutic mechanism in analytical psychology. See Chapter II and figures 5 and 6.

INFLATION

This describes the dramatic increase in energy experienced by a complex in some instances of psychic development. In the case of ego-identification with an archetype (e.g., mana personality), the archetype's store of libido (*numen*) is combined with the ego's; the result is figurative "inflation".

JOB, BOOK OF

Jung dealt in detail with this episode in the Bible as an illustration of religious expression of archetypal themes. The dual nature of God is clear in this story, as well as the essential unknowability of certain aspects of our psychological composition. Jung pointed out that the ambiguous experience with the unfortunate Job was the prelude to God's own individuation. See Chapter VI on the nature of Immanuel and Gandalf.

LAPIS

The stone, or philosopher's stone (*lapis philosophorum*) of alchemy illustrates the psychological potential of aspects of the form of dead matter and its inherent power: order, homogeneity, strength. The *lapis* is the mythical agent of transmutation of base metals into gold (q.v.), hence of transformation. As a special case, the *crystal* symbolizes order, symmetry, and perfection, hence the Self. References in Tolkien's work include the silmarils, Arkenstone, *palantíri*, Elfstone, star-forms, and Stone of Erech.

MANA

Mana is a Melanesian word denoting life-fluid or life-force. Jung used it in the same general sense as an attribute of psychic energy (libido).

MANA PERSONALITY

This peculiar case of inflation — usually an identification of the ego with the persona and consequent "pooling" of libido — is experienced in primitive (and not so primitive) cultures as a sense of burgeoning power and importance, an expansion of conscious will. This feeling is not particularly constructive; it often occurs during the individuation process after the first, inconclusive engagements with the anima(us), when such emotional chest-pounding is premature.

MANDALA

From Sanskrit: a magic circle used as a mantra in Tibet, generally round and symmetrical, often in conjunction with a cruciform design, hence associated with the similar concept of quaternity. Jung uses it as a symbol for self-centering. See Chapter II.

NEUROSIS

More correctly *psychoneurosis*, this term describes a general category of mental disorders characterized by a common symptom of anxiety (q.v.), with specific diagnoses based on additional symptoms. These may include hysterical "symptoms," dissociation, neurasthenia, phobias, obsessive-compulsive reactions, hypochondria, and related syndromes. In Jungian theory, neurosis is the result of psychic *one-sidedness* (q.v.).

NEGREDO

This is an alchemists' term which suggests the property of darkness; Cf. albedo, brightness.

NUMEN

Numen is a Latin word which derives from *nuere*, to nod in assent. It carries the meaning of divine will or divine power; Jung used it in the sense of libido or psychic energy bound up in a complex, especially in the unconscious. The related word *numinosum*, drawn from the same root, was used by Rudolf Otto in the context of group psychological possession by a mystical or emotion-laden (numinous) idea. This may be the origin of *Númenor*, Tolkien's name for the historical repository of Man's past greatness. (*Númen* = "west.")

ONE-SIDEDNESS

Overemphasis on conscious pursuits, to the exclusion of unconscious creative promptings, which amounts to denial of the nonconscious personal and collective personality, produces a figurative psychic energy-potential. This state of imbalance is called *one-sidedness*, and is associated with disorder in Jungian theory.

ORIGINAL MAN

Original Man, or Anthropos, is an archetypal figure in myth and religion, typified by the Judaic Adam and the Chinese nature god P'an Ku; the origin of life, of humanity, personified in the form of a primal ancestral image. See the discussion in Chapter VII of Bombadil as such a mythical figure.

OSIRIS

This Egyptian deity was the spouse of his sister Isis and brother of Set, all being the offspring of the Sun, Ra-Harakhti. In the rebirth cycle, Osiris was killed by Set and resurrected by Isis; their son Horus battled and defeated Set and the world of life was renewed. This was the basis for a yearly festival of renewal, which was at the center of Egyptian religious life; the sacred wedding of Osiris and Isis was revived in ritual with the marriage of the King, who was literally Horus in life and Osiris after death. The common strains of the renewal cycle are exemplified in the rebirth of Osiris and in other myths, in particular the resolution of the War of the Ring; see Chapter VIII.

PERSONA

This is the outward manifestation of the personality, the social "mask" (the name derives from the mask of classical drama). This outward personality may be unhealthy to the extent that it differs from the individual's true potentials and abets one-sidedness; the identification of the ego with the persona results in *inflation* of consciousness (q.v.). (Note, however, that the persona, aside from its possible inflation, is necessary to social adaptation.)

PERSONALITY

The process inferred from the sum of individual relations with others.

PERSONIFICATION

The endowment of a nonhuman thing with human attributes. The shadow may, for example, be personified in dreams as an animal or lurking human presence. In the process of individuation the anima (q.v.) is personified in the conscious and confronted by the ego. In dreams and myth, the anima may take the form of a wicked witch, temptress, or other feminine form; the she-bear served this symbolic function in Celtic lore. See the discussion of Shelob as the personification of the anima's negative attributes (Chapter VIII).

PROJECTION

This is a psychological mechanism by which internal attributes or motivations are "projected" onto an external agent. A man might project the image of his own anima on a woman, who would then (perhaps unwillingly) assume, in the beholder's eye, elements of his subjective Self.

PSYCHE

From the Greek ψυχή ("soul"); the totality of mental and spiritual processes.

PSYCHODYNAMIC

General title for a collection of theories, notably those of Freud, Jung, Adler, and several neo-Freudians. The common strand of these perspectives is the concept of personality as the outcome of an internal dynamic struggle between construct forces.

QUATERNITY

An archetype associated with the symbolic arrangement of things or ideas in fours or multiples of four; associated with the Self by virtue of the attributes of balance and perfection.

REGRESSION

In Freudian theory, regression is a backward chronological movement of behavior patterns, from mature to less mature ("regression to infantile behaviors"). Jung extends the Freudian context, describing it as a condition brought about by energic forces of archetypes attempting unsuccessfully to find expression in conscious symbols. When there are no such symbols available, the libido is said to *regress* into the unconscious.

REPRESSION

This is the defensive relegation of material which is threatening to or inconsistent with conscious requirements into the unconscious. In Freudian theory, repression is the primary mechanism of ego defense; in Jungian theory, repression occurs but its consequences are much more important than the process itself.

RUBEDO

In alchemy, the property of redness; see discussion of Narya, the Ring of Fire, in Chapter VI.

SCHIZOPHRENIA

Any of a wide variety of severe mental disorders with a common characteristic of psychotically disturbed thought processes. Influence of archetypal material is often observed in the verbal and artistic symbolism of schizophrenics, particularly in the paranoid and hebephrenic subtypes. See discussion of ego identification with archetypes and psychosis in Chapter VI.

SELF

This is Jung's term describing the potential controlling and organizing force of the personality. It differs from the ego in that it transcends conscious and unconscious strata. In the construct topography of the psyche the Self dwells at the midpoint, between ego and shadow. The Self is realized through the process of individuation (q.v.).

SEPTEM SERMONES AD MORTUOS

In *Seven Sermons to the Dead* Jung assumed the character of a Gnostic theologian of ancient Alexandria to ponder the nature of God, Man, and the psyche. This is a dauntingly abstruse work, interwoven of obscure Christian and pagan philosophy on the duality of God and Jung's individual conflicts. The compensating two-sidedness of the God of Gnosticism reflects, in Jung's view, the two-sidedness of the psyche.

SHADOW

The *alter ego;* the negative side of ego-consciousness, the invisible remnant of evolutionary heritage. Additional elements repressed by the ego cluster around it by association. See Chapter II.

SYMBOL

A symbol is the projection of an archetype into the conscious. Although the archetypal images remain the same, their symbolic vessels must change as the cultural context changes with time.

TELEOLOGY

The philosophical presumption of *goal-direction* rather than pre-determination of events by antecedent causes (determinism). Jung's theory is in many respects teleological, since the development of the personality is drawn by the potential of Self-realization rather than driven (as in Freud's theory) by infantile experience and in-nate sexual drives.

THEORY

A statement of relationships between processes or things (con-structs); theories are generally constructed to explain and/or predict events or processes.

TOTEM

An object or thing, often an animal, adopted as the symbol of a tribe or clan or, in the more modern context, a formal group. In Freudian theory, the totem is a projection of the father in indirect form, a vestige of the Primal Horde experience. In analytical psy-chology, groups may project the collective soul onto such an ob-ject, which then acquires a numinous quality. See the discussion of Beorn in Chapter VII.

TRANSCENDENT FUNCTION

This refers to the symbol-forming mechanism of the Self; the function that makes possible the progression of the maturing psyche from one-sidedness to two-sided balance and compensation. This is the strongest teleological aspect of Jung's psychic dynamic, called by von Franz the "symbol-forming spirit" upon which free communication between conscious and unconscious depends. (Franz, *C. G. Jung: His Myth in Our Time*, p. 96.)

TREE

The tree is a common symbol of psychic growth (instinctual growth being more often symbolized by animal figures or images). The tree is suggestive of life and growth, and particularly transcendence by virtue of its position joining heaven and earth, and the Self. The White Tree of Gondor fulfills this function in the War of the Ring.

TRICKSTER

The earliest form of the hero cycle, Trickster is usually a mythical figure, often of animal form, who survives and conquers by cunning rather than true wisdom. Folk heroes such as Br'er Rabbit and the Amerindian heroes Coyote and Raven are examples, as is Tom Bombadil in *The Fellowship of the Ring*.

UNCONSCIOUS

From the German *Unbewussten:* that part of the psyche which does not, except under unusual circumstances, intrude into awareness. In Jungian theory, there is a personal unconscious, which contains unique personal content, and the collective unconscious (q.v.), which includes collective experiences of race and species.

VESSEL

The vessel or container often symbolizes the feminine, being womblike in form. Vessel is also connected in symbolic context with divinity, as in the Grail legend, the vessel in this case being the repository of Christ's blood. See discussion of the vial of Galadriel and Sam's box in Chapter VIII.

VIRIDITAS

In alchemy, the property of greenness (Cf. albedo, rubedo, etc.). The color is associated with divinity, life, renewal, and reanimation. See discussion of the Elfstone in Chapter VIII.

WHITE GODDESS

The feminine principle appears many times in myth and religion, often in the context of the earth and its mysteries. In Semitic and European forms, this principle may appear as the White Goddess in a variety of forms. In Middle-earth the White Goddess is Varda, Kindler of Stars and spouse of Manwë. In the traditional fashion, Varda (Elbereth) watches over Middle-earth while Manwë averts his eyes toward the heavens. See discussion of Varda in the role of White Goddess in Chapter VI.

WISE OLD MAN

This archetypal image appears in many myths and fairy tales; the Old Man may be a guide and helper (hermeneut), the interpreter of mysteries.

WOTAN

Wotan (or Odin) was the one-eyed king of the *Aesir*, the Norse-Teutonic pantheon. The name associated with other archetypal forms, such as Wise Old Man, refers to affect-images of wisdom and daemonic power, sorcery and the seed of mayhem. We might characterize a powerful and aggressive warlord or dictator as "possessed" by Wotan; that is, the ego identifies with the Wotan archetype and so becomes dangerously inflated. See discussion of Saruman's predicament in Chapter VI.

YANG PRINCIPLE, YIN PRINCIPLE

The eternal opposites are named yin and yang in Taoism. One is light, the male principle, the heavens; the other darkness, the female principle, the earth. An eloquent if abstruse statement of this idea (albeit in Gnostic, not Taoist, terms) is to be found in Jung's *Septem Sermones ad Mortuos*. See discussion of the Mistress of the West (Varda) and Lord of the East (Sauron) in Chapter VI and of Elros and Elrond in Chapter III.

BibliogRAphy

Bodkin, Maud. *Archetypal Patterns in Poetry: Psychological Studies of Imagination*. London: Oxford University Press, 1963.

Bodkin, Maud. *Studies of Type-images in Poetry, Religion, and Philosophy*. London: Oxford University Press, 1951.

Brown, Arthur. *The Origins of the Grail Legend*. London: Humphrey Milford, and Cambridge, Mass.: Harvard University Press, 1943; reprinted New York: Russell & Russell, 1966.

Carpenter, Humphrey. *J. R. R. Tolkien: A Biography*. London: George Allen & Unwin, 1977.

Franz, Marie-Louise von. *C. G. Jung: His Myth in Our Time*, trans. William H. Kennedy. London: Hodder and Stoughton, 1975.

Freud, Sigmund, *Totem and Taboo*. London: Routledge & Kegan Paul, 1975.

Graves, Robert. *The White Goddess*. London: Faber and Faber, 1961.

Grimm, Jakob. *Teutonic Mythology*, trans. James Stalleybrass. London, 1883–88; reprinted New York: Dover Publications, 1966.

Hawkes, Jacquetta. *Man and the Sun*. London: The Cresset Press, 1962.

Henderson, Joseph, and Oakes, Maud. *The Wisdom of the Serpent: Myths of Death, Rebirth and Resurrection*. New York: George Braziller, 1963.

Jung, C. G. *The Collected Works of C. G. Jung*, ed. Herbert Read, Michael Fordham, Gerhard Adler, and William McGuire; trans. R. F. C. Hull. London: Routledge & Kegan Paul. Volumes used in this work are listed below:

5. *Symbols of Transformation*, 1980
6. *Psychological Types*, 1971
7. *Two Essays on Analytical Psychology*, 1967
8. *The Structure and Dynamics of the Psyche*, 1960
9. *The Archetypes and the Collective Unconscious*, 1980
10. *Civilization in Transition*, 1964
11. *Psychology and Religion: West and East*, 1970
12. *Psychology and Alchemy*, 1969
13. *Alchemical Studies*, 1968
14. *Mysterium Coniunctionis*, 1978
16. *The Practice of Psychotherapy*, 1970

Jung, C. G., ed. *Man and His Symbols*. London: Aldus Books, 1975.

Jung, C. G. *Memories, Dreams, Reflections*, ed. Aniela Jaffé; trans. Richard and Clara Winston. London: Collins, 1963.

Jung, C. G. *VII Sermones ad Mortuos*, trans. H. G. Baynes. London: Stuart & Watkins, 1967.

Jung, Emma, and Franz, Marie-Louise von. *The Grail Legend*, trans. Andrea Dykes. London: Hodder and Stoughton, 1971.

Noel, Ruth. *The Mythology of Middle-earth*. London: Thames and Hudson, 1977.

Perry, John. *Roots of Renewal in Myth and Madness*. San Francisco: Jossey-Bass, 1976.

Rychlak, Joseph F. *Introduction to Personality and Psychotherapy*. Boston, Mass.: Houghton Mifflin, 1973.

Sherif, Muzafer, and Sherif, Carolyn. *An Outline of Social Psychology*. New York: Harper & Bros, 1956.

Shumaker, Wayne. *Unpremeditated Verse: Feeling and Perception in Paradise Lost*. Princeton, N.J.: Princeton University Press, 1967.

Tolkien, J. R. R. *Farmer Giles of Ham and The Adventures of Tom Bombadil*. London: George Allen & Unwin, 1975.

Tolkien, J. R. R. *The Hobbit*. London: George Allen & Unwin, 1979.

Tolkien, J. R. R. *The Lord of the Rings*. London: George Allen & Unwin, 3 vols, 1976.

Tolkien, J. R. R. *The Silmarillion*. London: George Allen & Unwin, 1977.

Tolkien, J. R. R. *Tree and Leaf; Smith of Wootton Major; The Homecoming of Beorhtnoth Beorhthelm's Son*. London: George Allen & Unwin, 1975.

Tolkien, J. R. R., and Swann, Donald. *The Road Goes Ever On: A Song Cycle*. London: George Allen & Unwin, 1978.

Watts, Alan. *The Two Hands of God*. London: Rider, 1978.

Wilson, Edmund, "Oo, Those Awful Orcs!" *The Nation*, 14 April 1956.

index